The Town of Hercules

The Town of Hercules

**A BURIED
TREASURE
TROVE**

Revised and Expanded

Joseph Jay Deiss

THE J. PAUL GETTY MUSEUM ❖ MALIBU, CALIFORNIA

On the front cover:
The catastrophic A.D. 79 eruption of Mount
Vesuvius, as portrayed by the French
painter Pierre-Henri de Valenciennes in 1813.
(Detail from *The Death of Pliny the Elder.*)

Frontispiece:
A perfectly preserved life-size bronze statue
of a horse; recovered from the town of
Herculaneum. (Roman, first century A.D.)

On the back cover:
(upper left) Detail from an eighteenth-century
painting by Pietro Fabris.

(upper right) Fresco. Photo: Erich Lessing/Art
Resource, NY.

(lower left) Fresco depicting cupids playing
hide and seek. Museo Nazionale, Napoli,
Soprintendenza Archeologica delle Province
di Napoli e Caserta.

(lower right) Bronze statue of a horse.
Sorprintendenza Archeologica delle Province di
Napoli e Caserta.

Christopher Hudson *Publisher*

Mark Greenberg *Managing Editor*

Tobi Levenberg Kaplan *Editor*

Louise Mandell *Photograph Researcher*

Vickie Sawyer Karten *Designer*

Elizabeth Burke Kahn *Production Coordinator*

Dusty Deyo *Illustrator*

G&S Typesetters, Inc. *Typesetter*

Tien Wah Press *Printer*

Printed in Singapore

© 1995 The J. Paul Getty Museum
17985 Pacific Coast Highway
Malibu, California 90265-5799

Library of Congress Cataloging-in-Publication Data

Deiss, Joseph Jay.
    The town of Hercules : a buried treasure trove / Joseph Jay Deiss.
  — Rev. and expanded.
        p.   cm.
    Includes index.
    ISBN 0-89236-222-7
    1. Herculaneum (Extinct city)—Juvenile literature. [1. Herculaneum
(Extinct city)] I. Title.
DG70.H5D4   1995
937'.7—dc20   94-41648
                                                      CIP
                                                       AC

CONTENTS

Dedicated to every boy and girl

who ever wanted to find and dig up

a buried treasure.

"To come to know a fragment of our past is to recognize a piece of ourselves."

—Paul MacKendrick, classicist

INTRODUCTION

The story of the Town of Hercules begins in southern Italy, along the fertile, deceptively tranquil slopes of Mount Vesuvius.

It is difficult for most of us to imagine living at the foot of an active volcano, but many people do just that and seem to think nothing of it.

Near the city of Naples in southern Italy, thousands of people now live on the slopes of a volcano called Mount Vesuvius. Some residents occupy the simple one-story stone houses of their ancestors. Many more occupy modern ten- or twelve-story reinforced-concrete apartment houses. These people will tell you that they are not the least bit afraid of the volcano. Yet everyone knows that neither the old nor the new buildings are safe.

High on the volcano is a watchtower. There, scientists are on guard day and night, measuring every movement and taking the volcano's temperature at regular intervals. Lack of smoke and steam may indicate that internal pressure is rising. When the temperature goes up, warning alerts are issued.

With Mount Vesuvius looming in the background, the modern-day city of Ercolano (formerly Resina) crowds up against a small excavated portion of the ancient Town of Hercules.

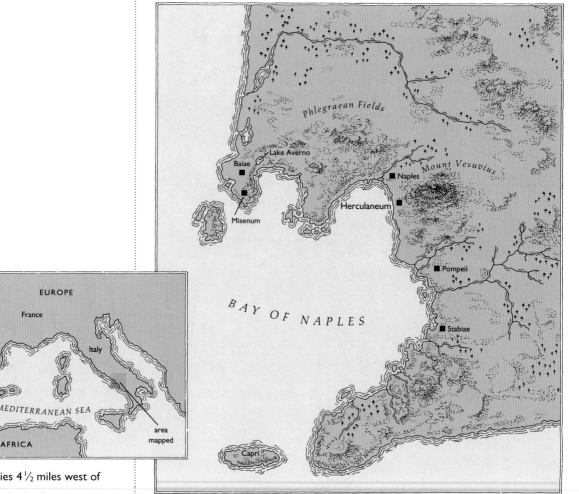

Herculaneum lies 4 ½ miles west of Mount Vesuvius. In the first century A.D., it was one of several towns scattered along the Bay of Naples in southern Italy. Small map (insert) shows the Bay of Naples region in relation to modern-day Italy and its surroundings.

The people say that they know the habits of "Vesuvio." They say that "he" always gives warning before one of "his" periodic eruptions. They tell tales of various eruptions and say that volcanic "grunts" are danger signals. Everyone believes that there will be time to run away before the next eruption does any real damage. But the truth is that volcanoes are not dependable. Very little accurate information about them exists. They date from when the earth was young, but only recently have scientists begun to understand what they are really like.

More dangerous than living at the foot of an active volcano is living near a volcano that is thought to be dead, but actually is not. Then the eruption—often a gigantic explosion—can come without warning and cause a major disaster.

That is what happened to the people who were living on the slopes of Mount Vesuvius nearly 2,000 years ago. Almost everyone thought that Vesuvius was an ordinary mountain. Only a few suspected that it was a dead volcano. Many little towns were spread beneath Vesuvius along the pleasant shore of the Bay of Naples. Today we know the details of two such towns: Pompeii and Herculaneum. These towns have been partially cleared of the volcanic matter that covered them when Vesuvius roared to life in the year A.D. 79.

Herculaneum was discovered before Pompeii, but it is not as famous. Of the two towns, Herculaneum proved much more difficult to uncover, but in many ways it is more interesting than Pompeii because it is better preserved. A visit now is almost like a visit to the living town of twenty centuries ago.

This book is the story of Herculaneum—the town of the hero-god Hercules. It is pronounced *her-cue-LAH-nay-um* in Latin, the language of the Roman people who lived there at the time of the great eruption. In the language of the people who live there now, the Italians, the name is Ercolano, pronounced *air-koh-LAH-no.*

Even 2,000 years ago, the people of Herculaneum, who were at that time citizens of the great Roman Empire, thought of their town as an ancient one—just how old, nobody knew. Like groups of people the world over, Romans told and retold special stories to explain events they did not understand. According to

> **KEY DATES**

700s B.C.   Oscans establish a village at what is now Herculaneum.

500s B.C.   Greeks settle in area around Bay of Naples and establish trading posts at Herculaneum, Pompeii, and elsewhere. Etruscans arrive in the region and compete with Greeks for control. Greeks defeat Etruscans to gain supremacy.

400s B.C.   Samnites invade the Bay of Naples region and eventually conquer the Greeks to become the dominant power.

400–290 B.C.   The Romans move in and fight three wars against the Samnites. Roman soldiers are victorious in the third war (290 B.C.). Herculaneum and other towns become "allies" of Rome.

90–89 B.C.   Herculaneum and Pompeii join an unsuccessful revolt against Rome. People of Herculaneum become citizens, with Latin as their official language.

A.D. 62   A strong earthquake damages Herculaneum and Pompeii.

A.D. 79   Mount Vesuvius erupts, burying Herculaneum, Pompeii, and other towns.

Green and lushly covered with trees and terraced vineyards, Mount Vesuvius was a symbol of life, not death, to the artist who painted it on a Pompeian wall more than 2,000 years ago. Bacchus, god of wine, stands guard wearing a suit of grape clusters. Today, grapes and wine continue to be important to the region's economy. The snake was the "serpent of the hearth," and meant good fortune.

one myth often told in Herculaneum, Hercules founded the town while returning from Spain, in the course of completing his twelve famous labors. Residents of the Town of Hercules believed this and many other legends, but their "true" history is a somewhat different, though no less fascinating, tale.

Long before Romans came to Herculaneum, other settlers and invaders were attracted by the region's gentle climate, fertile soil, and lush vegetation. Whether groups coexisted peacefully or fought hard to establish control, each contributed to the culture and history of the little seaside town and the surrounding region.

Who were the original founders of the Town of Hercules? Some scholars believe that, more than 2,600 years ago, a group of native people called Oscans set up a village on the beautiful high ground between two streams flowing down the slopes of Mount Vesuvius—right on the spot that would become Herculaneum. Oscans were hunters and fishermen who were probably descendants of the region's Stone Age dwellers. Their language was adopted by later peoples, and Oscan words and names appear on the excavated walls of Pompeii and Herculaneum.

In the sixth century B.C. (that is, from 500 to 600 years before the Christian era), Greek traders joined the Oscans and set up outposts at Herculaneum and elsewhere along the shore of the Bay of Naples. Greek culture and commerce thrived in the coastal towns and gradually replaced whatever Oscan civilization had existed. The logical pattern of Herculaneum's streets is just one indication of the town's Greek origins.

Next came the Etruscans, rich and powerful people from the area north of Rome, whose advanced civilization had widespread impact. These conquerors remain shrouded in

> THE STORY OF HERCULES

Legend has it that Herculaneum was founded by the brave and powerful hero-god Hercules, the town's special protector from earliest times. Hercules was a demigod (half-human, half-god). His father, Jupiter, was king of the Heavens and his mother, Alcmene, was a mortal. The goddess Juno, Jupiter's jealous wife, declared war on Hercules as soon as he was born.

The infant Hercules with Juno's serpents.

She sent two great snakes to kill the baby as he lay sleeping in his cradle, but Hercules laughingly strangled the serpents. When Hercules became a young man, Juno schemed to send him off on a series of desperate adventures that became known as "The Twelve Labors of Hercules."

In the first labor, Hercules faced a fearsome lion that had terrorized people living in a place called Nemea. The beast's hide could not be pierced by any weapon of stone, bronze, or iron, so Hercules fought and killed it with his bare hands. He skinned the lion using its own sharp claws. From then on, he wore the pelt or carried it with him always—to let everyone know he was the courageous youth who had slain the famous Nemean lion.

Throughout the course of eleven more labors and other famous exploits, Hercules overpowered monsters, beasts, and tyrants, and came to the aid of the poor and the weak. He was the ancients' superman, and readers who look up the tales of Hercules will enjoy reading about the seemingly impossible tasks he performed. No wonder the people of Herculaneum named their town after this hero-god. Boys in the Vesuvius area are still given his name: in Italian it is *Ercole*.

The story of Hercules was originally an ancient Greek myth (Greeks called him Herakles) later adopted by the Romans. Judging from the two statues portrayed here as well as other artwork, the Roman view of the popular demigod was much different from the Greek view.

As envisioned by the Greeks, Herakles (right) is a well-proportioned youth, gracefully holding his weapon

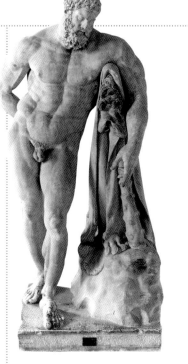

A Roman Hercules from the second or third century A.D.

of choice—the club—and his trademark lionskin. This ancient Roman adaptation of a Greek statue belongs to the J. Paul Getty Museum in Malibu, California.

In contrast, a Roman Hercules from the second or third century A.D. shows a bearded, middle-aged muscleman. He looks more human than godlike as he leans heavily on his club and lionskin. Although they revered Hercules, Romans seemed to enjoy mocking his human foibles and would sometimes portray him as a drunken bruiser in need of assistance.

The Greek view of Herakles.

mystery because their literature and history have been lost to us. During the sixth and fifth centuries B.C., the Greeks and Etruscans competed for supremacy in the region, with the Greeks triumphing.

The Greeks lost control of Herculaneum and the surrounding towns to the Samnites, fierce Italian clansmen from the mountainous interior region. These tough warriors spoke Oscan, the language of the first residents. They found the Bay of Naples irresistible and had soon adopted some of the trappings of Greek civilization, creating a kind of hybrid in which Greek culture flourished under Samnite domination. Samnite houses have been discovered at both Pompeii and Herculaneum.

Throughout the last half of the fourth century B.C., the ambitious Romans, seeking to expand their domain, attempted to conquer the entire region held by the Samnites. After many hard-fought battles over the course of three wars, Rome eventually prevailed. By 300 B.C., Herculaneum was under Roman control.

In 89 B.C., Herculaneum joined Pompeii and other cities in a revolt against the Romans. The attempt failed and both towns were quickly taken by the Roman army. Damage caused by the Roman siege engines may still be seen on the walls of Pompeii. Someday, when the town walls enclosing Herculaneum are uncovered, similar signs of the Roman battering may appear. After the siege, neither Pompeii nor Herculaneum had any need for the walls, because a long period of peace prevailed. With peace came prosperity. And with prosperity came the construction of large and beautiful townhouses and country estates, or villas.

The "Greekness" of Herculaneum persisted, but that was no barrier to the town's success with the Romans. All things Greek had become fashionable. All Romans spoke Latin, but many upper-class citizens spoke Greek as a second language. Roman buildings, art, and theater often copied the Greek. Romans renamed Greek gods and goddesses and adopted Greek religious practices. The craftsmen of Herculaneum were skilled in the Greek tradition. With its mild climate, beautiful location, and Greek origins, Herculaneum seemed perfect in Roman eyes.

From its tumultuous past, no one could have foreseen the future of dreamy little Herculaneum. No one could have guessed that it would become one of the most important cities in the world—all because of a sleeping volcano that awoke.

But first, many, many years had to pass.

1

A BUSY MORNING IN THE TOWN OF HERCULES

One day almost 2,000 years ago, grown-ups and children in this Roman seaside town were getting ready for a special summer festival.

Young Romans—like their elders—woke up at sunrise to make the most of the day's light. In Herculaneum, sunrise on August 24 in the year A.D. 79 seemed no different from any other dawn on a hot morning. Babies cried. Older children and grown people yawned, rubbed their eyes, and rolled out of bed as usual.

The Bay of Naples was blue and glassy calm. The mountain called Vesuvius was green with olive trees and vineyards. The sky was free of clouds and the sun was brilliant. It was a perfect day for swimming, boating, playing games, or hiking in the country.

The boys and girls of Herculaneum washed their faces in the cool water that flowed from the mountains in man-made channels called aqueducts. They put on their simple clothes, tied their sandals, combed their hair. Wild birds sang, and birds in cages answered. Lizards flicked long tongues at buzzing flies. Insects hummed and rasped in the tall, dark cypress trees. Here

This fresco, or wall painting, shows a Herculaneum mother, seated, overseeing her two daughters as they begin their day by carefully choosing what clothes and jewelry to wear. On the far right, a maid helps one of the young girls with her hair. These wealthy women are wearing thin fabrics in pastel shades—clothes for summertime—and have adorned themselves with lovely bracelets, necklaces, earrings, and rings.

Augustus, who ruled from 27 B.C. to A.D. 14, was the first Roman emperor. Coins like this one, with his face on it, let people all over the Empire see a likeness of their ruler.

and there a donkey brayed and a horse whinnied. The fishermen, who had set out to sea before dawn's light, were returning with a fine catch—fish, eels, squid. They were bringing their many-colored sailboats back to shore.

It was to be a busy morning in Herculaneum for everybody. First a simple breakfast was eaten: fresh fruit, cereal or bread with honey, milk or a little wine. Then teeth were cleaned. People went off to work, turned to their chores, and occupied themselves according to their age and class.

In August there was no school, so the younger children were free to run and play. Teenage boys worked as apprentices learning trades. Girls worked at looms or helped their mothers by caring for younger brothers and sisters. Sons of wealthy families were expected to study for a few hours under tutors, for education was considered very important. Boys of all ages were active in athletic events.

August 24 was known to Romans as the "ninth day before the Calends of September." On that day in A.D. 79, the Town of Hercules was in one of its gayest moods because, among other things, a festival was in progress. It was the celebration of the official birthday of the Emperor Augustus, a popular ruler who had brought new prosperity to the Roman Empire. After his death, some sixty years earlier, Augustus was deified. That meant Romans elevated him to the status of a god. The month of August was named for him.

The day before had also been a special one: a feast day in honor of Vulcan, the god of fire and metalworking. Romans believed that volcanoes were the chimneys of huge underground forges kept roaring hot by the fire god.

Outside the town gates, booths lined the roads, and all sorts of things were for sale. The vendors cried their wares aloud like hawkers at a carnival—sweets, pastries, melons in slices, grapes, coral charms, glass trinkets, sulphur matches, sandals and shoes, straw hats, tiny images of gods and goddesses. Townspeople were entertained by jugglers, acrobats, fortune tellers, and street musicians. Gamblers rolled dice or played the shell-and-pea game.

In celebration of the festival, Greek and Roman plays were advertised. Morning rehearsals were in progress at the Theater. In the sports arena, several athletic events were getting under way, and athletes would continue competing throughout the morning hours.

The streets of the town were jammed. The Forum was the busiest spot of all. Summer vacationers had come from Rome (the capital of the Empire situated to the north) and from Naples (a large, prosperous coastal city to the northwest). Peasants had come in from the country to see the sights. Poor women hurried to the public fountains, where they filled their terra-cotta jugs with fresh water. Each woman placed a jug on her head, balancing it on a coiled cloth. Rich women did not carry jugs; their houses had running water. In fact, they themselves were often transported around town in special chairs, called litters, borne by slaves. When they did walk outside, well-to-do ladies were protected from the sun's heat by parasols held by maids.

The snack bars had opened, offering bread of various kinds, cheese, wine, walnuts, almonds, dates, figs, and hot foods. Other shops displayed vegetables and grains, cloth, fishing gear, terra-cotta and bronze pots and jugs, glassware, bronze charms, and the handiwork of craftsmen and artists.

People in the Town of Hercules liked to gamble and play games of chance. The wall painting above (from a tavern in nearby Pompeii) shows a spirited dice game in progress.

The Bay of Naples provided a rich bounty of edible sea creatures. In this still life from Herculaneum, a lobster, several clams, and two cuttlefish surround a beautiful silver vase and small bird. The trident (a staff with three prongs) symbolizes Neptune, the Roman god of the sea.

In the stone relief to the right, customers crowd a shop selling everything from chickens (hanging on the wall) and rabbits (in a hutch, bottom right-hand corner) to bread and produce, displayed in baskets on the counter. A pair of monkeys quietly watch the lively transactions. (From a second-century A.D. shop sign found in Ostia, the port of Rome.)

A simple gold serpent ring rests against a small wooden box that might have been a jewel case. Both were found at Herculaneum.

Workers were busy, too. In the small workshops all sorts of things were being made. Cabinetmakers were putting together expensive inlaid wooden chests and furniture—hammering, sawing, turning their lathes. Artists called mosaicists were creating large pictures using pieces of glass and glazed stone smaller than a fingernail. The dyers of cloth were busy at their vats. The cloth press, a machine with a huge wooden screw almost as large as a man, was in full operation. Goldsmiths and silversmiths were at work on jewelry and dishes. Marble workers were cutting, carving, and polishing marbles of many different colors. An artist was painting a group of cupids on a piece of wood to be set into a plaster wall. A woman completed a sewing job and neatly tucked her thimble and needle in her basket.

Inside the elegant houses overlooking the waterfront and the sea, late-rising ladies were being dressed by their slaves. They had plentiful supplies of combs, hairpins, hair ornaments, mirrors, cosmetics, and perfumes. The ladies' jewel cases contained necklaces, bracelets, anklets, earrings, brooches, and rings, all made of gold and silver and set with precious stones.

In late morning the heat mounted. At the bakery of a

man named Sextus Patulcus Felix, the baker and his helpers prepared to take from the oven the bronze pans containing cakes and tarts. That the cake dough would rise during baking was assured both by the baker's skill and by a magic emblem over the door of the oven. Not far away, at another bakeshop where only bread and dog biscuits were baked, flour was being ground by two donkeys no bigger than large dogs. Wearing blinders, the donkeys walked in an endless circle turning the heavy stone mill. They continually flicked their tails and ears against bothersome flies.

At a metalsmith's shop a workman was heating his forge with a bellows, getting it good and hot so he could melt the nearby ingot of metal and begin repairing the broken objects sitting on his countertop.

Near the Forum, at the shrine of the deified Emperor Augustus, the priests were holding a meeting. Within the shrine, in a small barred and locked room, a man flung himself on a bed in despair.

At the shop of the gem cutter, a sick adolescent boy lay upon a finely made wooden bed. The boy was unable to get out of bed, so chicken was brought to him to tempt his appetite. Close to him, a woman worked at a small loom, weaving cloth. As she worked she probably urged the boy to eat so that he might get well quickly.

The men's section of the public baths had opened. Slaves helped the earliest comers to undress. Clothing was folded and placed on stone shelves running along three of the walls. To make the water hotter, other slaves were stoking the boiler and raking out ashes with a long iron poker. At the more luxurious Suburban Baths overlooking the marina, the steam room and hot and cold bathing areas were already in operation. Young

Tradesmen and shopkeepers were hard at work on the morning of August 24. At this metalsmith's shop, a worker was getting ready to fix the small bronze statue of Bacchus and the large bronze candlestick waiting on the counter. He set out two ingots of metal next to Bacchus and began heating up the forge with a bellows—but never managed to make the repairs.

D A V I D

"David" probably used a stick, a writing tool, or maybe even a nail to scratch his name onto a Herculaneum wall some 2,000 years ago. He was just one of many people—boys and girls, young and old, rich and poor—who left personal messages on walls throughout the town. In their scribbles, notes, names, and lists, we can almost hear the voices of Herculaneum's residents speaking to us across the centuries.

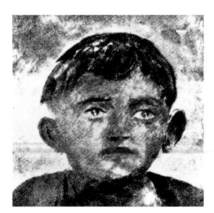

This portrait from a Pompeiian wall painting brings you face to face with a sad-eyed Roman child.

men in one of the rooms had drawn some less-than-flattering pictures of their friends on a white plaster wall, along with a collection of bawdy verses.

In fact, all over town boys had drawn pictures and written their names on walls. Some of them were Marcus and Rufus and Sabinus and Manius and Florus and Julius. Older girls, like one named Virginia, wrote about love, or how much they missed their boyfriends. A boy named David wrote his name on the wall of a Roman house. Unlike the others, David must have been a Jewish boy. His name is a Hebrew, rather than a Roman (or Latinized), name.

Toward noon, the athletic events in the arena were nearing completion. Boys who were victorious in the stone toss, and perhaps swimming, were preparing to receive their olive-wreath crowns. They were naked and deeply suntanned, for Roman athletes, like Greek athletes, did not wear clothing. The victors' crowns were spread out on a broad marble table in the great hall.

The playing field of the sports arena was surrounded by a columned walkway. In the center of the field, an olympic-size swimming pool in the shape of a cross sported a giant bronze serpent spraying water from five crowned heads. Officials, guests, and special fans sat in a shaded balcony on the north side, protected from the sun's glare. They rose and cheered the winners.

In almost every house, lunch was being prepared. Wooden tables were set in shaded courtyards or gardens with fountains splashing. Romans preferred a light lunch. At an imposing house built above the marina, waiters were about to serve hard-boiled eggs, bread, salad, small cakes, and fruit. Whole loaves of fresh bread, baked in round pans, had been placed on tables throughout Herculaneum. At one house, lunch was a little early—the bread had been broken and set down on the tablecloth. After lunch, during the hottest part of the day, the people of Herculaneum would take a long afternoon nap.

Near the Forum, a shipment of expensive glassware had just arrived. The glass was of beautiful design. It was packed in a special case carefully stuffed with straw. So eager were the owners to see their newest treasure that lunch was postponed while a servant began to open the case. The first protective layer of straw was torn away.

Suddenly, a violent cracking sound split the air. The earth heaved and shook. It sounded as if the ear-shattering roars of a gigantic bull were coming directly out of the earth. The yellow sunlight abruptly disappeared. In its place, an unnatural overcast sky appeared. From the mountaintop a vast cloud in the shape of a mushroom billowed up into the sky.

Crazed with fright, dogs barked and cats ran into hiding. People screamed that Vesuvius had blown apart. All who could rushed wildly into the streets.

One of the greatest and most terrifying natural disasters of all time had begun.

Round loaves of bread were set out on tables throughout the Town of Hercules as people got ready for their noonday meal.

2

THE VOLCANO EXPLODES

When Pliny the Younger was seventeen years old,
he was an eyewitness to the devastating eruption of
Mount Vesuvius. Years later, he vividly described the
event in two remarkable letters.

Warnings had not been lacking, but people had paid little attention. For some days mild earthquakes had been felt in the whole region of the Bay of Naples. The town of Pompeii, 10 miles away on another flank of Vesuvius, had felt the shocks. The great city of Naples, farthest from the mountain, had felt them too. But in this zone they were not at all unusual: A major earthquake seventeen years earlier had caused a great deal of damage. People had become used to feeling occasional earth tremors, and so were caught completely by surprise when the tremors were followed by a cataclysmic volcanic eruption.

It is astonishing that so few reports of the disaster have survived from antiquity. The only eyewitness description is that of Pliny the Younger, who was a teenager at the time. Years later, as a forty-two-year-old man, he wrote two letters to the Roman historian Tacitus. Tacitus wanted to know the story of the death of young Pliny's famous uncle, the naturalist known as Pliny the Elder.

Pliny the Younger wrote that Mount Vesuvius hurled "a horrible black cloud ripped by sudden bursts of fire" into the sky. "It writhed snakelike and revealed sudden flashes more intense than lightning." Eighteen centuries later, a French painter created this view of what the thunderous explosion might have looked like to young Pliny's uncle and his slaves. (Detail from *The Death of Pliny the Elder*, Pierre-Henri de Valenciennes, 1813.)

Pliny the Younger as an adult.

To Pliny the Younger, the massive eruption cloud resembled "a tree—the
umbrella pine would give the best idea
of it. Like an immense tree trunk it was
projected into the air and opened out
with branches." Umbrella pines like the
one here—displaying its classic form
in front of Mount Vesuvius—are still a
familiar sight throughout Italy.

Shortly before the eruption, Emperor Titus had
appointed Pliny the Elder commander of the Roman fleet
of ships based at the little town of Misenum, a port on the Bay
of Naples. It was even farther from Vesuvius than Naples. The
Pliny family had a large country house, or villa, at Misenum.

Young Pliny was very fond of his uncle, who had
become his adoptive father after his own father's death.
Although he wrote with restraint, he conveyed powerful
emotions and images. His letters are masterpieces. In the first
one he wrote:

My dear Tacitus—You ask me for an account of
my uncle's death, so that you may hand on a more reli-
able report of it to future generations. Thanks for this. I
am sure that your report will make certain that he is
never forgotten.

He was at Misenum in command of the fleet.
On the ninth day before the Calends of September
[August 24] at about the seventh hour [shortly after
noon], my mother informed him that a cloud of extraordinary size and appearance had been seen. He had
finished sunbathing, taken his cold bath, and lunched
and was at work on his books. He then called for his
sandals and climbed to a high point for the best possible view of the remarkable event.

The cloud was rising. Watchers from our distance
could not tell from which mountain, though later it
was known to be Vesuvius. In appearance and shape it
was like a tree—the umbrella pine would give the best
idea of it. Like an immense tree trunk it was projected
into the air and opened out with branches. I believe

that it was carried up by a violent gust, then left as the gust faltered. Or, overcome by its own weight, it scattered widely—sometimes white, sometimes dark and mottled, depending on whether it bore ash or cinders.

It was natural that a man of my uncle's scientific knowledge would decide that so grand a spectacle deserved close study. He ordered that a light galley be made ready. He gave me the opportunity of going with him if I wished. I answered that I would rather study, as he himself had assigned me some homework to do. Just as he was leaving, he received a note from [his friend] Rectina, Caesius Bassus's wife, . . . begging him to save them from their peril. Now he saw his expedition in a new light. What he had begun in the spirit of a scientist, he carried on as a hero.

He boarded ship with the intention of rescuing not only Rectina but others as well—for the charm of the coast had attracted many people. So he hastened in the direction from which others were fleeing, setting the helm for a course straight into the danger. Yet he kept so calm and cool that he noted all the changing shapes of the cloud, dictating his observations to his secretary.

And now ashes were falling on the ship, thicker and hotter the closer they approached. Also pumice stones and cinders—blackened, scorched, and scattered by the fires. Shallows suddenly were encountered, and landing was made difficult because the shore was blocked by rubble from the mountain. The pilot urged that they turn back. My uncle hesitated. Then he said: "Fortune favors the brave—steer toward Pomponianus!"

This man Pomponianus lived at Stabiae, on the

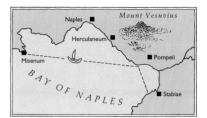

Pliny the Elder sailed from Misenum to observe the eruption and rescue as many people as he could. His friend Rectina had sent a desperate plea for help, so the Admiral first tried to land near her villa south of Herculaneum. But floating rafts of fallen ash made it impossible for his ships to reach the shore. He continued on and was able to land at Stabiae, where another friend, Pomponianus, lived. The next morning Admiral Pliny died on the beach at Stabiae.

far side of the bay (for the sea thrusts in between curving shores). There the danger was not yet immediate, though very near and very evident as it increased. Pomponianus had collected all his movables on shipboard, with the intent to sail the moment the opposing wind died down. My uncle, favored by this same wind, reached land. He embraced his anxious friend and cheered and encouraged him.

To calm fear by an appearance of unconcern, he asked for a bath. Then after bathing he sat down to eat with gusto, or at least (no less admirable) making a pretense of gusto. From Mount Vesuvius, meanwhile, great sheets of flame were flashing out in more and more places. Their glare and brightness contrasted with the darkness of the night. My uncle, to relieve his companions' fears, declared that these were merely fires in farmhouses deserted by their peasants.

Then he lay down and slept. His sleep was unmistakable. His breathing was heavy and noisy because of his bulk and was heard by those who listened at the door. But the courtyard on which his room opened was being choked by a rising layer of cinders and ash. If he delayed any longer it would have been impossible to escape. So he was wakened and went to join Pomponianus and the others, who had not slept.

They discussed whether to remain in the house or to go outside. The walls of the house were swaying with repeated violent shocks. They seemed to move in one direction and then another, as if shifted from their foundations. Nevertheless, everyone dreaded the rain of pumice stones, though small and light, in the open air.

In this engraving from 1888, a downpour of ash and volcanic debris send panic-stricken townspeople scrambling to safety. At Stabiae, Pliny the Elder and his companions tied pillows to their heads in a feeble attempt to avoid injury from a similar onslaught.

After discussion they chose the second of the two dangers. My uncle was moved by the stronger reasons, and his companions by the stronger fears. With strips of linen they tied pillows to their heads and went out.

Elsewhere day had come, but there it was night—a night blacker and thicker than any ordinary night, though relieved by torches and flares of many kinds. They decided to go down to the shore, to see at first hand whether it was possible to sail. But the waves continued very rough and contrary.

There my uncle lay down on a sailcloth that had been cast ashore. He called repeatedly for water, which he drank. Then the approaching flames and the smell of sulphur put the others to flight. Aroused, my uncle struggled to his feet, leaning between two slaves. Immediately he fell down again. I assume that his breathing was affected by the dense vapors and that his windpipe was blocked. (It was weak, and often inflamed.)

When daylight returned, on the second day after my uncle had last seen it, his body was found. It was intact, without injury, and clad as in life. He seemed asleep, not dead.

Meanwhile Mother and I were at Misenum. But that is not to the purpose, as you did not want to hear anything more than the facts of his death. So I will conclude.

But Tacitus did want to hear more. Pliny wrote a second letter, about what happened at Misenum:

After my uncle's departure, I gave the rest of the day to study, the object that had kept me at home. Afterward I bathed, ate dinner, and went to bed. It was a short and broken sleep.

For several days we had experienced earth shocks. They hardly alarmed us, as they are frequent here. That night they became so violent it seemed the world was not only being shaken but turned upside down. My mother rushed to my bedroom just as I was rising. I had intended to wake her if she was asleep. We sat down in the courtyard of the house, which was separated by a short distance from the sea. Whether from courage or inexperience, I called for a book and began to read. I even continued writing in my notebook, as if nothing were the matter. . . . Though it was the first hour of the day, the light appeared to us still faint and uncertain.

Though we were in an open place, it was narrow. The buildings around us were so unsettled that the collapse of walls seemed a certainty. We decided to leave town to escape this menace.

The panic-stricken crowds followed us, responding to that instinct of fear that causes people to follow where others lead. In a long close tide they pushed and jostled us. When we were clear of the houses, we stopped, for we met fresh terrors. Though our carts were on level ground, they were tossed about in every direction. Even weighted with stones they could not be kept steady.

The sea appeared to have shrunk, as if withdrawn by the shaking earth. In any event, the shore had widened. Many sea creatures were beached on the sand. In the other direction loomed a horrible black cloud ripped by sudden bursts of fire. It writhed snakelike and revealed sudden flashes more intense than lightning. . . . Soon after, the cloud began to drop down upon the earth and cover the sea. Already it had surrounded and hidden Capri and blotted out Cape Misenum.

My mother now began to beg, urge, and command me to escape as best I could. A young man could do it. She, burdened with age and heaviness, would die easy if only she had not caused my death. I replied that I would not be saved without her. Taking her by the hand, I hurried her along. She came with reluctance, and not without self-reproach for getting in my way.

Ashes began to fall, but at first sparsely. I turned around. A frightening thick smoke, spreading over the earth like a flood, followed us. "Let's go into the fields while we can still see the way," I told my mother. I was afraid we might be crushed by the mob on the road in the darkness.

We had scarcely agreed when we were enveloped

in night. Not a moonless night or one dimmed by cloud, but the darkness of a sealed room without lights. To be heard were only the shrill cries of women, the wailing of children, the shouting of men. Some were calling to their parents, others to their children, others to their wives, knowing one another only by voice. Some wept for themselves, others for their relations. There were those who, in their very fear of death, prayed for it. Many lifted up their hands to the gods. But a great number believed there were no gods—that this night was to be the world's last, eternal one.

A curious brightness revealed itself to us not as daylight but as approaching fire. It stopped some distance from us. Once more, darkness and ashes, thick and heavy. From time to time we had to get up and shake them off for fear of being actually buried and crushed under their weight.

I can boast that in so great a danger I did not utter a single word or a single complaint that could be considered a weakness. I believed that one and all of us would die—that made my own death seem easier. But the darkness lightened, and then like smoke or cloud dissolved away. Finally a genuine daylight came. The sun shone, but faintly as in an eclipse. And then, before our terror-stricken gaze, everything appeared changed. Everything was covered by a thick layer of ashes, like an abundant snowfall.

We returned to Misenum, where we refreshed ourselves as best we could. We passed an anxious night between hope and fear—though chiefly fear. The earthquakes continued. Even so, my mother and I, despite the danger we had experienced and the danger which still threatened, had no thought of leaving until we should receive some word of my uncle.

Eventually Pliny the Younger and his mother received the sad news. The Admiral indeed had met his death from Vesuvius.

The grim extent of the destruction must have astonished Pliny the Younger when he sailed out into the Bay of Naples. The panorama of that beautiful shore had completely changed. From Herculaneum to Stabiae not one town could be seen. All was covered by gray ash and cinder, no longer lush with palms, flowers, grapevines, and olive trees. The volcanic flows had created a new shoreline that extended far out into the sea. It was steep and forbidding.

In the background loomed Vesuvius, with a lazy plume of smoke drifting skyward.

3

WHAT REALLY HAPPENED

How accurate was Pliny the Younger's account? Today, scientists read the story of the volcano's eruption in layers of deposits that have been preserved through the centuries.

Pliny was the first known person to describe the step-by-step behavior pattern of a volcano from the beginning of an eruption to its end. His letters have been of great help to modern volcanologists (scientists who study volcanoes) as they examine layer after layer of the volcanic fallout laid down by Vesuvius. By comparing their findings with Pliny's letters, volcanologists like Haraldur Sigurddson and his colleagues have concluded that the story coded in ancient deposits closely matches the deadly sequence of events described by Pliny the Younger.

Pressure had been building deep beneath the earth's surface for a long, long time. Earthquakes and ground tremors provided some release, but not enough. At around one o'clock in the afternoon of August 24, A.D. 79, enormous geologic forces reached the bursting point. With a thunderous crack, the whole top of Vesuvius blew off. Traveling at twice the speed of sound, super-hot ash, pumice, rocks, and gases shot straight up,

Mount Vesuvius lights up the sky during a 1771 eruption. The volcano has delivered more than fifty violent explosions since Pliny's time. (From an eighteenth-century painting by Pietro Fabris.)

The Roman emperor Titus, shown on a coin minted in the year A.D. 80, came to power less than two months before the eruption of Vesuvius. After the disaster, he provided relief for the survivors and assigned special commissioners to investigate ways to help the ruined district.

high into the stratosphere. Twelve miles above the earth, the plume fanned out into a large cloud.

Pliny described this blast cloud in great detail and compared its shape to that of a local tree, the umbrella pine. Today we might say it resembled an atomic mushroom cloud. This type of volcanic event has become so closely associated with Pliny that volcanologists now use the term *Plinian eruption* to describe the explosive mushroom-shaped cloud.

For the next eighteen hours, the volcano continued to erupt. The huge blast cloud blocked out the midday sun. The cloud's contents were released on the bay and countryside below.

As it happened, the wind was blowing southeast—toward Pompeii. Throughout the afternoon and evening of August 24, some 8 feet of hot ash, pumice, and stones fell on the town of 20,000 people. Terrified victims were struck down by buildings collapsing under the weight of all the volcanic material. A few people were injured or killed by red-hot projectiles. Many Romans thought, like Pliny, that it looked as if the world were coming to an end, and they fled from the infernal rain of volcanic debris. Before it was all over, more than 12 feet of ash and pumice would blanket Pompeii, and 2,000 people would die there.

Herculaneum, lying upwind 4½ miles west of the volcano's cone, received only a light dusting of ashfall during the first twelve hours. With the erupting volcano in full view, many frightened residents of the Town of Hercules no doubt hurried off to Naples, Rome, and other safer places. Those who remained in town—or anywhere within a few miles of the cone—didn't stand a chance. The Plinian phase was ending, but Vesuvius had something worse in store.

At about one o'clock in the morning, with the night sky

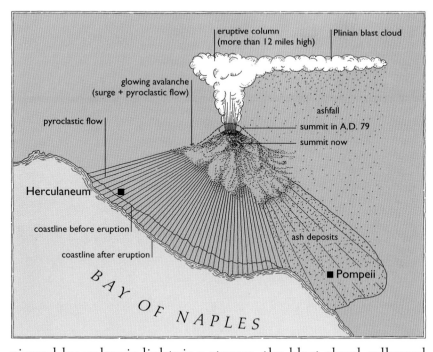

eruptive column
(more than 12 miles high)

Plinian blast cloud

glowing avalanche
(surge + pyroclastic flow)

pyroclastic flow

ashfall

summit in A.D. 79

summit now

Herculaneum

coastline before eruption

coastline after eruption

ash deposits

Pompeii

BAY OF NAPLES

When Mount Vesuvius erupts, winds blow the ash-laden blast cloud away from Herculaneum and toward Pompeii. Twelve hours later, a series of six deadly glowing avalanches overwhelm and bury the Town of Hercules—and permanently extend the shoreline farther out to sea. Two avalanches reach Pompeii.

pierced by volcanic lightning storms, the blast cloud collapsed under its own weight. A violent storm of hot gas and ash hurtled down the flanks of Vesuvius at speeds of up to 100 miles per hour. This glowing avalanche, a turbulent, 750-degree-Fahrenheit hurricane of volcanic material, reached Herculaneum in just four minutes. There was no time to run and nowhere to go. The volcanic storm killed every living thing in its path.

As it advanced, the glowing avalanche separated into two stages: the faster, gaseous surge cloud and the slower, ash-laden pyroclastic flow. ("Pyroclastic" comes from two Greek words: *pyros*, "fire," plus *klastos*, "broken," so the word means "fire fragments.") The hot, front-running surge raced through the town, ripping tiles off roofs and turning dry wood into charcoal as it traveled down to the beach and boat chambers. Searingly hot gases in the cloud immediately killed the townspeople who had sought shelter there. As the surge barreled

> THE ERUPTION'S VOLCANIC DEPOSITS

During the first day, Herculaneum (opposite page) received only a light dusting of ash, but in the middle of the night it was attacked by the first of six glowing avalanches. Each avalanche consisted of two phases: a lethal, boiling-hot surge made up of ash and gases, and a denser, ground-hugging pyroclastic flow. The surge, though deadly, left a thin, inconspicuous layer for future scientists to study, but the pyroclastic flow deposits are hard to miss: They account for most of the 65-foot accumulation that buried the Town of Hercules.

Pompeii (below), located downwind of Vesuvius, was buried under 12 feet of airborne ash. The volcano's fourth surge and flow was the first glowing avalanche to reach Pompeii. In human terms, the glowing avalanche did more damage than the massive ashfall. Striking on August 25 at 7:30 A.M., it killed every one of the 2,000 people still in the city.

- ☐ ashfall deposits
- ■ surge deposits ─┐
- ☐ pyroclastic flow deposits ─┘ *together glowing avalanche*

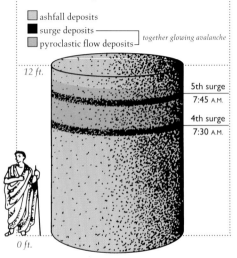

12 ft.

5th surge
7:45 A.M.
4th surge
7:30 A.M.

0 ft.

Pompeii

into the Bay of Naples, seawater boiled and threw off steam explosions. The more liquefied pyroclastic flow followed close behind. It oozed into the large sports arena and filled the cross-shaped swimming pool, then flowed down the town walls and out along the beach—permanently extending the shoreline.

Those people who had stayed behind were quite dead now, but Vesuvius continued hammering away at Herculaneum with the deadly one–two punch of surge and pyroclastic flow—burying the town deeper and deeper. The glowing avalanches came six times in all. Each wave traveled at a different speed, and some flows were hotter than others. They ranged from 6 to 9 feet in thickness. Just as the ashfall had, each surge and flow left a clear record, a marker, for future volcanologists to study. Ironically, the deposits left by surges are thin and unimpressive—even though they are the deadliest, most destructive phase of an eruption.

Pompeii, crippled and devastated by ashfall, had not yet experienced the full fury of the eruption. But at seven-thirty on the morning of August 25, a glowing avalanche—Vesuvius's fourth—rolled over the 6 to 8 feet of accumulated ash to kill the unfortunate souls who still remained in that doomed city.

With its sixth and final surge, Vesuvius caused the death (probably by heart attack) of young Pliny's uncle, Pliny the Elder, who collapsed on the beach at Stabiae. Pliny the Younger described this surge, the volcano's most powerful display, as a "horrible black cloud ripped by sudden bursts of fire [that] writhed snakelike." He didn't realize it had taken his uncle's life.

The glowing avalanche could be called the knockout blow of an eruption. It is not the same as lava, which is red-hot liquid rock. Lava moves so slowly that a person can outrun it. True lava was not produced by Vesuvius during this eruption. In Herculaneum the pyroclastic flows seem to have followed the stream beds. Some flows moved with such speed and force that entire houses were swept away, large statuary was toppled, and massive columns were tilted or overthrown. Other flows oozed slowly. The semicircular Theater was filled to the brim like a huge bowl, then overflowed. Tables were left still set for lunch, oils lamps hung from their brackets, and documents in some houses were still legible 2,000 years later. Graffiti on many walls remained as readable to modern eyes as when they were first scrawled with chalk or pen. Bread and grains, walnuts, rope, fishnets, even toys escaped destruction.

It is amazing that so much has been preserved in spite of the high temperatures of some of the flows. With modern scientific methods it has been possible to estimate that some wood in Herculaneum was heated as hot as 752 degrees Fahrenheit. (If the town had been buried by true, red-hot lava, everything would have been melted or burned to ashes.) Most amazing of all, bodies of the dead remain, their skeletons intact. But this a subject for another chapter.

By the end of the eruption, Herculaneum had been buried to an average depth of more than 65 feet. The town's shoreline had been pushed 1,500 feet farther out to sea. The volcanic matter hardened into a type of stone called tufa that now can be sawed or chiseled away to reveal the town and its contents.

The dreadful news of the eruption was flashed to Rome by a series of signal towers, the Roman way of telegraphing. At once the Senate declared the whole region a "disaster area," just as we do today. The popular emperor Titus used his own funds to

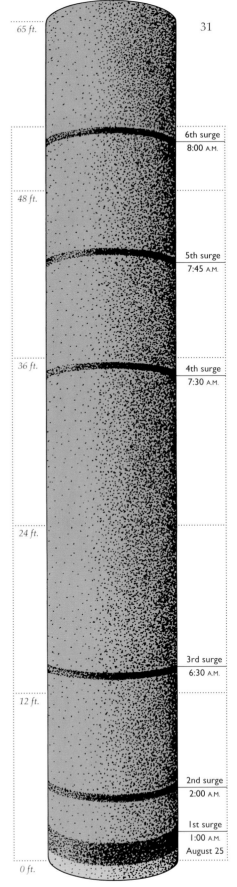

65 ft.

6th surge
8:00 A.M.

48 ft.

5th surge
7:45 A.M.

4th surge
7:30 A.M.

36 ft.

24 ft.

3rd surge
6:30 A.M.

12 ft.

2nd surge
2:00 A.M.

1st surge
1:00 A.M.
August 25

0 ft.

Herculaneum

AUGUST 24

1:00 P.M.   Eruption begins. A 12-mile-high Plinian blast cloud towers over the region.

1:30 P.M.   Ash and red-hot chunks of rock begin to fall on Pompeii and entire downwind region.

2:30 P.M.   Pliny the Elder sets sail from Misenum.

5:30 P.M. Buildings begin to crumble in Pompeii.

AUGUST 25

1:00 A.M.   Plinian eruption cloud collapses. Within minutes, a glowing avalanche kills all townspeople left in Herculaneum.

1:00–6:30 A.M.   Three more deadly surges and flows hurtle down the flanks of Vesuvius.

7:30 A.M.   A glowing avalanche reaches Pompeii and destroys every living thing in its path.

8:00 A.M.   Volcano's largest surge occurs. Alarmed, Pliny the Younger and his mother join a frantic mob fleeing Misenum; Pliny the Elder dies at Stabiae.

help provide relief. He came from Rome to speak with survivors. A few people tried to dig out the lost towns, without results. No aid could make up for so total a disaster. The towns seemed buried forever by Vesuvius.

In death, Herculaneum left behind a daily record of its life 2,000 years ago. The record is more complete there than at any other site from antiquity explored by archaeologists. The town was sealed as if in plastic—a time capsule preserved for us to study today.

Vesuvius has become the world's most famous volcano, and the most studied. It seems incredible now that people in the area did not recognize its volcanic origin. Only a few had eyes sharp enough to see. Many years before Vesuvius erupted, the geographer Strabo climbed to the peak of the mountain and remarked that it looked like a "spent" volcano. Other clues in the area were overlooked.

For example, in the Bay of Naples area, continuous volcanic activity could be found. Only 20 miles from Herculaneum itself were the famous Phlegraean Fields. This real place was known then, as now, for its smoking caverns and geysers of steam and water. At the infernal Lake Averno, the waters that filled an extinct volcanic crater were as black as those of Hades. Hot mineral waters gushed from the earth at the fashionable resort called Baiae and also at Stabiae, near Pompeii. Luxurious baths were built by the Romans at both places, and the modern town called Castellammare di Stabia is still an impressive spa with many mineral springs.

Yet in A.D. 79 no one could have guessed that Vesuvius had been born 17,000 years earlier and had exploded in at least four

major eruptions before the one that destroyed Herculaneum and Pompeii. No written record or story of any eruption had come down to the ancient Romans. Today, however, volcanologists are able to study the geologic record—the layers of volcanic deposits laid down by Mount Vesuvius. These layers, or strata, tell us that after A.D. 79 Vesuvius roared to life more than fifty times. Although very little is known about most of the eruptions, we do know that in the year 203 the volcanic explosion was heard many miles away. In 472 and 512, blasts were preceded by severe earthquakes, heavy lava flows, and great glowing clouds of ash that were carried over several countries. In 1139, Vesuvius erupted for eight days.

The volcano's worst eruption of the twentieth century to date lasted for eighteen days in April of 1906. Mountains of ash that fell on the Vesuvian town of Ottaviano were hauled away by horse-drawn carts.

The last time Vesuvius erupted was 1944. Amid grunts and roars, the volcano hurled stones—some as large as basketballs—a distance of many miles.

On December 16, 1631, Vesuvius exploded with a violence that rivaled even the A.D. 79 display. Many villages were destroyed—including one that was swallowed whole. Naples was covered by a thick coat of ashes. The town of Resina, built atop the buried and forgotten Herculaneum, was nearly demolished. By the end, 4,000 people and 6,000 farm animals had lost their lives. After the eruptions of 1760, 1771, and 1794, better records were kept, including drawings and paintings of the events.

In the modern period, beginning in 1858, Vesuvius continued to make its presence felt. It erupted in 1861, 1872, 1906,

1929, 1933. Its most recent eruption occurred in 1944, just as Allied troops were landing in Italy during the war against Nazi Germany—in World War II. At that time, instruments had just been developed that could detect the coming eruption. The Allied Military Command took many photographs and prepared a detailed report (which was not released until 1970). Observers said the volcano grunted like a huge beast and tossed stones the size of a man's head.

After the Roman period, the names and locations of Herculaneum, Pompeii, and the other buried towns were forgotten. For many, many years it was as if they had never existed. Then came an accidental discovery that changed both history and the science of archaeology.

Once again, Herculaneum and Pompeii began to come to life.

> **MOUNT ST. HELENS**

Perhaps what happened to Vesuvius can be better appreciated by looking at the 1980 explosion of America's own Mount St. Helens, shown here spewing an eruption of steam, ash, and hot gases 11 miles into the air.

■ The blast leveled all forests within 15 miles, hurling trees as if they were sticks. Tons of pumice and searing rock were thrown into the air.

■ An enormous landslide completely filled a large lake; 150 million tons of ash choked rivers at their sources.

■ Survivors said, "In an ash storm you can't breathe. The inside of your mouth is burned, you hear your hair sizzle. But your clothes are hardly scorched. It's like a burn from a microwave oven."

4

THE LOST TOWN AND HOW IT WAS FOUND

Vesuvius the Destroyer became Vesuvius the Preserver, burying the Town of Hercules so completely that it remained sealed and untouched for sixteen centuries.

Human memory, even for disasters, is short. With passing time, not only the sites but even the names of the buried cities were forgotten. The writings concerning Herculaneum, Pompeii, and other local towns were destroyed or lost. Even the nine published volumes of young Pliny's letters disappeared. Three hundred years after the eruption, the Roman Empire began to crumble in the face of barbarian invasions from the north. A great decline had begun, and it lasted for many centuries.

The carefully constructed buildings of Rome were destroyed or fell apart stone by stone. Marble was burned to make lime. Bronze was melted for weapons. Magnificent statues of Roman and Greek gods were destroyed by pious Christians. Temples were converted into churches or pulled down. Aqueducts that for centuries had carried clear mountain water to the cities for drinking water and baths were cut by the invaders, and city people were forced to drink and bathe in

At Herculaneum, pyroclastic flow covered everything, then cooled and hardened into solid rock. Laborers in the 1920s use pickaxes to excavate two-story buildings along one of the town's streets. A specially built narrow-gauge railway hauls away piles of debris.

> KEY DATES

A.D. 79   Mount Vesuvius erupts violently for two days, completely burying the Town of Hercules. Eventually, knowledge of the lost town's existence fades from memory.

1503   A map shows roughly where Herculaneum is located.

1709–1716   While digging a well, workers accidentally discover ancient marble. An Austrian prince mines the site for buried treasure.

1738   Workers discover an inscription identifying the Theater and the town of Herculaneum. Looting continues under King Charles III, who appoints a Spanish military engineer named Alcubierre to oversee excavations.

1750s   The Villa of the Papyri, a lavish country house outside Herculaneum, is discovered. Karl Weber, a Swiss architect, explores and maps the buried Villa.

1765   All excavations are halted at Herculaneum and the Villa of the Papyri. Tunnels are sealed. Focus of explorations shifts to Pompeii, where digging is easier.

dirty river water. Marshes were no longer drained. Mosquitoes spread, and with them, malaria. Libraries were ransacked. Christians burned the greatest library of the ancient world, in Alexandria, Egypt. Rome's famous Forum, once a thriving center of commerce, became instead a place where goats grazed and pigs rooted.

During the periods of Western history known as the Dark Ages and the Middle Ages (from roughly the 470s to the 1300s), many people lived in filth, ignorance, and misery. The skills of Roman craftsmen—like bricklaying—were no longer passed from generation to generation. The science of medicine slid further into witchcraft.

After more than a thousand years, people began to find inscriptions and sculptures from the Roman past. Educated people became interested in the art and literature of the ancient world, and a kind of "antiquity fever" set in. Old books were found in the monasteries—and people read them. New interest arose in Roman and Greek literature, sculpture, and architecture. The Renaissance—the "re-birth"—had begun.

Somehow a geographer learned of the existence and location of Herculaneum. In 1503, he marked it on a map that was almost accurate. On the lower slopes of Vesuvius, the fertile volcanic soil was once again planted with vineyards, orchards, and olive trees. A new town named Resina was built right on top of the buried city of Herculaneum. The people who lived in Resina had no idea that an ancient city lay under their feet.

Despite the map, Herculaneum's long sleep was not to be disturbed until the 1700s. Misfortune—in the form of another devastating eruption—mingled with luck in the strangest way to lead to the town's discovery. The powerful eruption of Vesuvius in 1631 that had nearly destroyed the town of Resina had also wreaked havoc on the vineyards, gardens, and water supply in the surrounding countryside. During the long period of rebuilding, a few Roman coins were found and rumors of ancient buried treasure began to circulate. Then, in 1709, workmen digging a well for a monastery near Resina brought up not water but rare and beautiful polished marble.

It happened that an Austrian nobleman, Prince d'Elboeuf, was building a luxurious villa nearby. He needed marble, so the find was called to his attention. The Prince realized that the well-digger had stumbled upon an important structure dating from antiquity. He cared nothing for the building itself, or for the ancient people once associated with it. He was interested only in what he might find there for his own project.

He ordered workers to deepen the well and to dig exploratory tunnels. All sorts of marvelous discoveries were made, including life-size marble statues of three women. The plunder continued for as long as the Prince's villa was under construction, a period of seven years. Finally, Prince d'Elboeuf gave up his treasure hunt and left Herculaneum to its gravelike peace. The Prince never realized that he had made one of the most important archaeological strikes of all time. He did not know that he had been looting the ancient Theater of the long-lost Town of Hercules.

In the early 1700s, when Herculaneum and then Pompeii were rediscovered, archaeology—the study of ancient peoples—did not exist as a rigorous scientific discipline. In fact, the growth of this young field parallels the almost 300-year history of

> **KEY DATES**

1828–1835, 1852–1855 Francis I, King of Naples, renews explorations; two more blocks are excavated.

1869–1875 King Victor Emmanuel II sponsors the final excavations of the 1800s. All work stops when local landlords fear for the safety of Resina's buildings. Giuseppe Fiorelli oversees excavations at Pompeii, pioneers new methods.

1927–1960 Modern excavations proceed under Amedeo Maiuri.

1960–1970s Under Alfonso de Franciscis, General Superintendent of Antiquities in the region around Naples, excavations, conservation, and restoration continue.

1982 Workers discover the skeletal remains of more than a hundred victims of Vesuvius inside boat chambers and along the ancient seafront.

1990s Intermittent exploration and restoration continue as money and politics permit.

King Charles III of Spain was a teenager
when he began sponsoring excavations
at Herculaneum.

archaeological excavations around Mount Vesuvius. At Herculaneum, what began as a haphazard hunt for valuables slowly evolved into a more orderly effort to learn about ancient civilization. New methods, new ideas, new goals changed the way men and women approached Herculaneum and Pompeii. Different people were in charge of excavations at different times, and each new leader influenced the form and outcome of each new dig—and advanced or hampered the development of archaeology itself as a science.

The Austrian prince who looted Herculaneum for its precious marble and statues was the first of many players in the long story of the town's journey from darkness to light. The next major figure was a teenager. Charles III of Spain was nineteen years old when he became king of Naples in 1734. (This was before Italy was one nation.) He and his young bride were interested in the buried treasure trove in southern Italy. They wanted to raid it to decorate their palace.

The young king appointed not a scholar but a Spanish military engineer to begin digging. He could hardly have made a worse choice for an archaeologist or a better one for a treasure hunter. The engineer, a man named Rocco Gioacchino de Alcubierre, enlarged the original shaft of the well. He made a gaping hole, letting in daylight on a few of the Theater's upper seats. He enlarged existing tunnels into galleries and began new tunnels in all directions.

In 1738, the Theater that had been discovered almost thirty years earlier was finally identified. Shortly afterward, an inscription was found that proved the site was Herculaneum. At last the Town of Hercules would return to the map. It would bring new finds of dramatic appearance and great value. Sculptures, objects, and paintings were carried to the Royal Palace of

> A PASSION FOR ANTIQUITIES

Pompeian Room.

Wedgwood plaque.

During the 1700s and 1800s, excitement about the discoveries at Herculaneum and Pompeii captured the imagination of people throughout Europe and in America. Lured by the prospect of peeking through a window to the distant past, artists, writers, architects, and tourists visited the sites of the buried cities.

Charles Dickens, the famous author of *Great Expectations*, *A Christmas Carol*, and many other works, explored Vesuvius in the mid-1800s. Dickens was excited and fascinated by the thought that "house upon house, temple on temple, building after building, and street after street are still lying underneath, . . .

waiting to be turned up to the light of day."

Inspired by what they saw, many artists, potters, and architects incorporated Greek and Roman motifs in their work. Ancient designs began to appear on everything: jewelry, vases, lamps, sets of silverware and dishes, even entire buildings. In the 1770s, Josiah Wedgwood created decorative ceramics displaying scenes from Pompeii and Herculaneum that remain popular to this day. In the 1780s, Thomas Jefferson designed silver objects based on what he had seen during a trip to Italy. And a lavish "Pompeian Room" was built at Buckingham Palace in 1844, six years after Queen Victoria visited an excavation site at Pompeii.

How difficult is it to dig through solid rock? Royal treasure hunters working for King Charles III of Spain found out the hard way. In the mid-1700s, they hacked out this underground excavation tunnel to explore the buried Town of Hercules. Their progress was slow and dangerous.

King Charles III. This was the beginning of the collection that eventually was to rest in the National Archaeological Museum in Naples, where it can be seen today.

The military engineer, Alcubierre, was guilty of many stupidities. For example, he removed bronze lettering from walls and statue bases without first reading the inscriptions. The result was a heap of meaningless letters that looked like alphabet soup. Everything was haphazard. Digging was done on a whim, first one way, then another. Luckily, daily reports were issued, and a diary was kept in Spanish. But no record of the details of each find—its place, position, relation to other objects—was kept. No street plans or building plans were made. With convicts as laborers, crews burrowed everywhere: along streets; over roofs; through walls, wooden doors, vaults, paintings, and mosaics.

Alcubierre continued mining, smashing, and snatching until 1750, when a new person was finally appointed to help oversee the work. Karl Weber, a young Swiss architect, introduced some order into the chaos. For several years he had the opportunity to continue his more systematic tunneling, but he faced serious obstacles. One was the petty rivalry and opposition of Alcubierre, who told the king lies about Weber's progress and went so far as to remove scaffolding so that galleries would collapse. The other obstacles came from the nature of the site.

Workers had to hack their way down through 20 to 60 feet of hardened volcanic material—the solidified pyroclastic flow deposits. They were excavating solid rock. Earth and rubble were carried away in little straw baskets. The passages, deep underground, were just like dangerous mine shafts. Water and slime dripped from the walls. The work was slow and hazardous.

Gases constantly threatened workers with suffocation. The only light came from feeble oil lamps or smoky torches that made normal sculptures take on horrible "devilish" shapes. No wonder that little knowledge was gained of the general character of the town. All in all, the physical work of the early diggers was truly a thirteenth labor of Hercules.

Weber's efforts were rewarded later that year, when well-diggers came upon a richly decorated villa just outside the Town of Hercules. Working in dark underground tunnels, Weber spent fifteen years exploring the Villa of the Papyri. He

Giuseppe Fiorelli ushered in a new approach to archaeology as Director of Excavations at Pompeii in the 1800s.

Amedeo Maiuri directed the "modern" excavations beginning in the 1920s.

took careful notes, made drawings, and created a detailed floor plan. The Villa created a sensation when it was found and has continued to inspire people through the course of three centuries. It has never been completely excavated and remains buried to this day. Chapter 15 discusses the impact of this great archaeological discovery in detail.

In 1765, all tunnels were closed and all digging stopped. Interest shifted to Pompeii. It was easier and safer to dig there, and exciting new finds had occurred. People were after quick rewards of gold and silver and statues. No one was interested in investigating an ancient city for its own sake to find out how people had lived long ago.

More than sixty years later, another king of Naples became interested in Herculaneum. Young Francis I was deeply moved by Pompeii. Moody and romantic, he loved to take moonlight strolls among the ruins. He began to brood about the town buried under the suffocating mass of volcanic rock. In 1828, he ordered a renewal of digging at Herculaneum.

King Francis felt that Herculaneum ought to be brought out into the open. He ignored the tunnels and began working in an area that did not lie under the crowded streets of Resina. Hacking away with great effort at the solidified matter with hand tools, progress was slow. Eventually, though, a few houses were uncovered. People began to speak of ancient Herculaneum as if it were an ordinary Italian town.

After seven years of the new attempt, the results did not seem equal to the efforts. Digging methods were so crude that the ancient houses were wrecked as they were revealed. They appeared as almost total ruins. Rich finds were rare. So the king

The entrance foyer to one of Herculaneum's public baths shown during and after excavation. In the far left photo, a small statue and basin are still encased in the volcanic rock that has kept them perfectly preserved for nineteen centuries.

After the hardened material has been chipped away bit by bit (near left), a fine bust of the god Apollo is revealed. Pipes inside the statue's base carried a flow of water that continuously splashed into the fountain's marble basin.

lost interest, and the project was dropped in 1835. From 1852 to 1855 exploration briefly resumed, and a Roman snack bar and some shops were explored before digging was once again abandoned.

For fourteen years, neither pick nor shovel was seen at Herculaneum. Excavations finally resumed in 1869, under united Italy's King Victor Emmanuel II. But the physical conditions of work—pitting strong arms and backs against the resistant stone—had not improved. Again progress was slight. As the digging approached the jumbled houses of Resina, a new difficulty arose: the flinty opposition of Resina's landlords. They were not interested in the knowledge gained through archaeology. They preferred the crowded slums of the present to the elegant but empty houses of the past. In 1875, Resina's property owners brought the excavations to a standstill.

Meanwhile, work had been progressing at Pompeii. From 1860 to 1875, Giuseppe Fiorelli, a pioneer of modern archaeological methods, was in charge. Until Fiorelli's appointment, excavations around Vesuvius were characterized by plunder rather than orderly exploration. Fiorelli changed all that. He viewed the ruins as a different type of treasure trove. Where others saw only objects of beauty and value, Fiorelli saw a wealth of information. Information about ancient Romans—their art, their politics, their culture, their way of life. Fiorelli imposed a rigorous plan for unearthing the city block by block. He insisted that new finds—whether of gorgeous wall-size frescoes or everyday household objects—be left in place. That way, people could see houses that were furnished and decorated, and visitors could appreciate works of art in their original settings.

Fiorelli's vision of a city brought back to life became something future archaeologists embraced, at Pompeii and Herculaneum as well as at other sites around the world. But the Town of Hercules would have to wait for another fifty years to pass before that vision would be even partly achieved there.

Work did not begin again at Herculaneum until 1927—a full 218 years after its initial discovery. Archaeology had grown from a hobby into a science. New machines. New methods. And a new man: Amedeo Maiuri, someone steeped in the tradition of Fiorelli. Maiuri used all of the technical tools of modern archaeology as he set about the task of returning the Town of Hercules to the light of day . . . intact.

The pioneering work of Maiuri and his successors accomplished a great deal. In many ways the Town of Hercules has lived up to its promise. Homes of rich and poor have been painstakingly restored. Great public places—the Baths, the Palaestra (a sports center or gymnasium), the Basilica (the courthouse)—have been explored. During the 1960s and

In the 1970s, students from many countries gathered each summer to volunteer their services with pick and shovel. Dubbed the "Herculaneum Academy," they toiled steadily under the blistering sun and helped sort and classify bits of pottery and other small finds.

1970s, Maiuri's successors limited their new excavations and concentrated on conserving and restoring buildings that had already been exposed. Today, perhaps more than half of the city remains buried, waiting to share its secrets.

In the early 1980s, one of the town's long-kept secrets suddenly became public knowledge. Workers (supervised by then-director of excavations Giuseppe Maggi) were digging a drainage ditch where Herculaneum's ancient marina used to be. By chance, they made a grim discovery: the intact skeletons of human victims of Vesuvius. Chapter 6 takes a look at how those skeletons influenced what experts now believe about the last days and hours of Herculaneum, and how their discovery has added to our knowledge of people and life in Roman times.

The list of equipment and specialists employed during the last seventy-five years amazes those of us who have no training in archaeology. How these tools would have astounded the early tunnelers: Clinometer for measuring slopes. Plane

In the 1990s, excavators turned their attention and expertise to the boat chambers fronting the ancient marina.

table for measuring angles. Alidade for showing degrees of arc. Prismatic compass for taking accurate bearings. Leveling staves marked in centimeters for measuring elevations. Templates for recording the curves of moldings. Brooms, brushes, and masons' tools for cleaning architectural finds. Zinc plates and sodium hydroxide pencils for electrolysis of coins. Measuring tapes of all sizes. Mechanical drawing instruments. Trowels. Marking pegs. Cord. Squared paper. Filter paper for taking "squeezes" of inscriptions. Catalog cards. India ink. Shellac. Cardboard boxes. Small cloth bags. Labels. Journal books, field notebooks, and technical manuals. Cameras. Picks, shovels, refuse baskets. Sonar equipment. Computers.

For a major dig like Herculaneum, even more equipment is needed: Compressed-air drills. Electric saws. Bulldozers. Narrow-gauge railway. Dump trucks and related equipment.

For stabilizing and restoring damaged buildings and ancient objects: Professionally trained conservators. Skilled masons. Mosaicists. Fresco painters. Marble workers. Bronze casters. Carpenters. Cabinetmakers. Chemists, for analyzing content of jars and bottles, paints, and kitchen pans. Metallurgists, for analyzing corroded or mixed metals. Glass experts. Physicists, for dating with the radioactive isotope Carbon 14. Historians, for their knowledge of background history. Language scholars—at Herculaneum, experts in Latin, Greek, Oscan, and, occasionally, Egyptian and Etruscan.

We may be grateful today that the early treasure hunters had so little success in uncovering the Town of Hercules. Their crude attempts to raid the site for ancient loot could have completely destroyed what the pyroclastic flow had preserved for centuries.

5

REVISITING HERCULANEUM

Thrown open to the light of day after 1,900 years of darkness, the excavated portion of the Town of Hercules gives us a glimpse of ancient Roman life.

Modern excavators have the aim of restoring the town to its original appearance. Archaeologists would like to think that a citizen of Herculaneum, magically returning after almost 2,000 years, would be able to find his house much as he left it— familiar objects all in place, food in the cupboard, flowers blooming in the courtyard, fountains running. Of course, creating a faithful reconstruction of the town is very hard to do.

With a little imagination, we can visualize a great deal about Herculaneum. If we had approached from the sea on that fateful August morning in the year A.D. 79, we would have seen a charming little town. First we would have noticed the sunlight glittering on gilded bronze statuary mounted on impressive public buildings. Then the deep greens of cypress, palms, and oleanders in the shady gardens would have caught our attention. Drawing closer, we would have seen a cluster of varied buildings, statues, and fountains along the marina, with the mansions of well-to-do families looking down from above.

Today, the rich red and gold hues of Herculaneum's ancient houses seem to glow among the lush Mediterranean greenery.

A bird's-eye view of the Town of Hercules shows the limited extent of modern excavations.

Beyond them, we would have spied the houses and shops of ordinary townspeople lining the streets.

Everybody asks, "How big was Herculaneum?" The answer is that nobody really knows. The population estimate of 4,000 to 5,000 is based on the number of seats in the Theater. The size of the area covered by the town remains unknown because only a small portion has been explored. Archaeologists have estimated the town's area at about 55 acres, but we won't know if that figure is accurate until the town has been completely excavated.

The town plan (what we know of it so far), with its orderly rectangular blocks (called insulae), is similar to that of

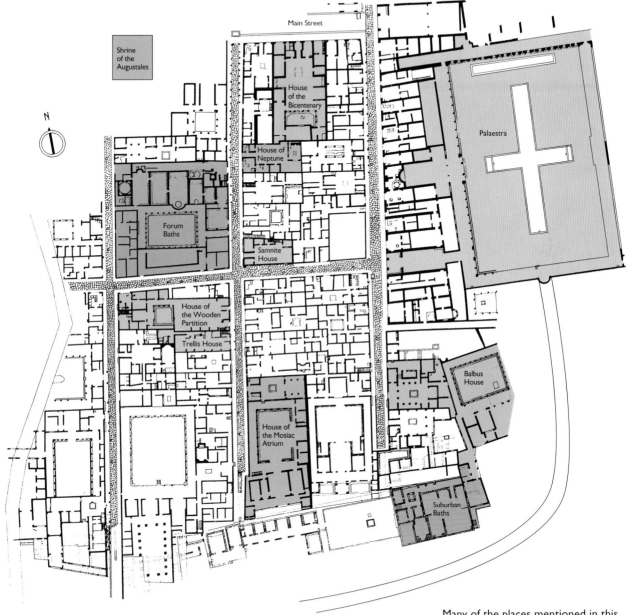

Main Street

Shrine
of the
Augustales

N

House
of the
Bicentenary

House of
Neptune

Forum
Baths

Samnite
House

Palaestra

House of
the Wooden
Partition

Trellis House

Balbus
House

House of
the Mosiac
Atrium

Suburban
Baths

Many of the places mentioned in this
book are highlighted on an updated
excavation map of Herculaneum.

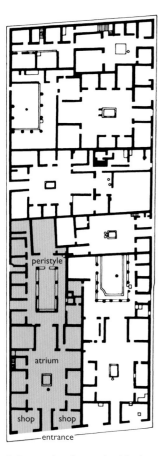

A Roman insula, or city block, consisted of houses and shops packed tightly together. There were no "backyards" as we know them. Instead, walls and columns created courtyards and gardens that brought fresh air and sunlight inside the houses. Shaded area indicates one large home.

ancient Naples, a city founded by the Greeks. Therefore, Herculaneum may also be Greek in origin. Volcanic stone called tufa, is still used in Naples, paved Herculaneum's streets.

Herculaneum's thoroughfares are different from those of neighboring Pompeii. Streets in the Town of Hercules rarely show ruts worn by wheels of heavily laden carts, and no stepping-stones were built to keep pedestrians' feet dry. Stepping-stones were not needed in Herculaneum because the town was equipped with an excellent drainage system. A large underground sewer carried wastewater and rainwater out to sea. Pompeii lacked such a sewer. These clues suggest that Herculaneum was a quieter and cleaner town than Pompeii. It was a place where people could go about their business along well-kept, well-drained streets, undisturbed by the noisy clatter of wheeled vehicles. At Pompeii, household garbage and sewage washed down the middle of busy streets. No wonder high sidewalks and stepping-stones were essential there.

Herculaneum's ample water supply flowed from the mountains through aqueducts built by the Romans. The town's water tower ensured that water pressure was adequate, and a filtration system purified the water so that it was safe to drink. Most modern cities would be fortunate to have water equally pure. Some houses had private wells and cisterns (storage tanks). They were not connected to the public water-supply system.

Many homes did not have their own bathrooms, and many Romans used public facilities. Although the public latrines have not yet been located, no doubt they were like other Roman latrines. That is, they probably had handsomely decorated rows of marble seats and were flushed with a constant flow of water. Romans did not feel the need to conceal natural body functions, so separate stalls were not built. Latrines in private homes either received a constant flow of water or could be flushed with a bucketful of water.

The private houses of Herculaneum are more advanced in their design than most of those in Pompeii. Houses were important possessions in both towns. They were built to last—not for generations, but for centuries. Houses were designed for a single family, its dependents, and its heirs. Often, homes were updated by changing the layout or the decorations—by remodeling. Apparently, Romans liked old houses, but not old-fashioned ones.

The basic Italic house followed a regular form. On the outside, it was simple and spare, with few windows or embellishments. This was to keep people from peering in and to deter burglars. A short entranceway (the fauces) led to the main room, a sort of central hall called the atrium. The roof, which sloped inward from all four sides, had an opening in the center (the compluvium) that let in both sunlight and rainwater (and in earlier times let smoke from the hearth escape). A pool or basin (the impluvium) directly below caught the water. Beyond the atrium was the tablinum, sometimes used as the main bedroom but often converted to a reception room or office. The kitchen, the dining room (the triclinium), and small, windowless bedrooms were located around the atrium.

In Herculaneum, old-style houses like the one described above were often greatly changed. They were so "modernized" that we would find them comfortable houses to live in today. Some had second stories with rooms upstairs. Many had a large, beautifully planted garden with an open colonnade of columns (a peristyle). With splashing fountains and a pool,

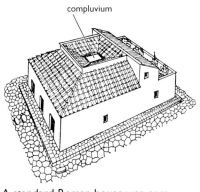

A standard Roman house was organized around the atrium. The opening in the roof (compluvium) allowed rainwater to flow into the pool beneath it (the impluvium). For security, exterior walls had few windows and narrow doorways, but, thanks to the compluvium, the house's interior was filled with natural light.

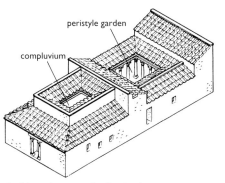

In Herculaneum, the basic plan was changed and embellished to create a variety of customized houses. The modified atrium house illustrated here has a large peristyle garden at the back with rows of columns and additional rooms—bedrooms, sitting rooms, even dining rooms.

> FUN AND GAMES

Teenagers joining in a lively ball game.

Roman grownups and children enjoyed some games that have been popular for thousands of years. Boys and girls played blindman's buff, leap-frog, board games, and—like the cupids in a Herculaneum wall painting—hide and seek. Everyone seemed to enjoy ball games, and all sorts of balls were used. The enthusiastic group of players shown in a Roman tomb painting have set up a goal and are throwing a medium-size ball.

Toys from the Town of Hercules look eerily familiar: the head from a child's doll, a black-and-white game board, playing tokens, and dice. Adults played "chess" and "backgammon," and were especially fond of gambling, using either dice or animal bones called knucklebones.

Mosaic game board and playing pieces.

Young women using animal bones for a gambling game.

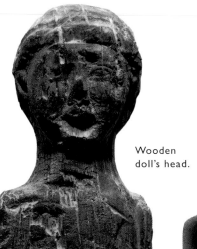

Wooden doll's head.

Cupids playing hide and seek.

Wooden dice.

the cool, pleasant peristyle garden provided an outdoor space within the privacy of the house. In the homes of some wealthy residents in Herculaneum, peristyle gardens were designed to take advantage of refreshing sea breezes and lovely views.

Herculaneum also had a large apartment house several stories high as well as a cheaply constructed house typical of the type built to meet the needs of the Roman population explosion.

The successive layers of pyroclastic flows that overwhelmed Herculaneum performed several important functions for which archaeologists are very grateful. In Pompeii the upper portions of houses collapsed under the weight of ash. But in Herculaneum the upper portions were supported. It is possible to walk along a sidewalk shaded by the overhanging upper stories of buildings that look almost exactly the way they did 2,000 years ago.

Much wood seems untouched. Stairs and shutters, tables and beds have been preserved. Herculaneum proves that the amount of wood used in ancient buildings was much greater than formerly supposed. It also shows us just how expertly made ancient Roman furniture could be.

The modern excavations have revealed additional information about the people of Herculaneum. They were much engaged in fishing, if the volume of nets, hooks, floats, and other gear is any sign. The shops, snack bars, and taverns were in plentiful supply, as might be expected in a seaside resort town. Also, many skilled craftsmen produced and sold their wares. In the back streets of Naples their descendants are still to be seen: wrought-iron workers, wood carvers, mosaicists, gilt

This 2,000-year-old bronze water valve from Herculaneum still works. The piece with the hole drops into the foot-long fitting below it and is turned to either stop or allow water to flow through the pipe. Pure water for drinking and bathing was brought from the mountains through stone aqueducts.

An amazingly well-preserved net is one indication of the importance of fishing to the town. The bronze tools on the right were used to repair damaged nets. Today, Italian fishermen maintain their nets using plastic instruments of the same design.

applicators, goldsmiths, and silversmiths. Finds of familiar-looking toys and game pieces indicate that Romans enjoyed many of the same games and leisure pastimes that we do today.

Attitudes toward love and sex are revealed in the paintings and statuary that people chose for their houses and gardens. The scribbles on the walls (graffiti) tell us even more, because Romans and Greeks were uninhibited. In many contexts, nudity was not considered improper or shocking. Athletes competed in the nude, and Romans looked forward to enjoying their communal baths each day. In paintings, men are portrayed as deeply bronzed by the sun, women as untanned and light-skinned. Scenes and situations frowned on by puritans were enjoyed by Herculaneans, who enjoyed sexual jokes.

Their point of view was one of easygoing naturalism. Even the most sexually explicit scenes were displayed in public—on shop signs, walls, paintings, bellpulls, jewelry, dishes, and statuary. Almost all forms of love were accepted as normal.

All human behavior was reflected in the gods themselves. Roman gods displayed human emotions, virtues, and vices. Their stories were told in paintings on hundreds of walls, and often in statuary.

We don't know a great deal about the organized religious life of Herculaneum, but we do know that religion was important to Romans of that day. They worshiped many different gods, or deities, including those of the people they conquered. Early Romans believed that gods and goddesses, demigods (half-human, half-god), and powerful spirits were everywhere and controlled human actions. When they worshiped—by offering prayers and sacrifices and by performing special rituals—they hoped to bring themselves good fortune by pleasing the gods. Romans prayed at private altars in their homes as well as at public temples and shrines.

In a typical Herculaneum home, statuettes of the household gods, the lares and penates, were kept on a shelf or in a shrine or niche (the lararium) located in the atrium. Sometimes pictures of the household's guardian spirits were painted on the wall. They represented the spirit of the house itself and the spirits of the ancestors. Devout Romans made daily offerings to them—a portion of food and drink.

Although Romans built many temples (in the city of Rome itself there are hundreds), not one temple has been discovered in Herculaneum. Perhaps future excavations will reveal a temple to the protecting god Hercules, for it must surely exist somewhere in the town. The only religious structure found so far is the beautiful Shrine of the Augustales, on Main Street. This sanctuary was built to honor the popular

The top of this cupboard from the atrium of a house in Herculaneum is a small shrine (lararium) containing statuettes of the lar and the penate. These "household gods" looked after the well-being of the family and guarded the home. Devout family members prayed at the altar every day and burned bits of food there as sacrificial offerings.

The base of the cabinet was used to store nonreligious objects—a dish of garlic and some glassware are visible.

The mark on the wall appears to be the remains of a Christian cross. Many scholars believe that this Herculaneum room, with its wooden cabinet and minimal furnishings, was a Christian chapel. If so, it would have been one of the very first in the Bay of Naples region, and the first known use of the cross as a Christian symbol.

Emperor Augustus, who was proclaimed to be a god (deified) after his death.

Statuettes of gods and goddesses have appeared in abundance: Jupiter (king of the gods), Bacchus (god of wine), Mercury (the messenger), and, in many forms, Venus. One particularly graceful life-size marble statue of Venus shows the goddess of beauty and love wearing a thin garment, expertly handled by the sculptor.

A haunting wall painting of white-robed priests of Isis performing their rituals demonstrates the Roman willingness to embrace "exotic" religions. Isis was an Egyptian goddess with a cult following among Romans. The mysteries of death and resurrection were an important part of worshiping her.

And what of Christianity, which was a brand-new religion in the first century A.D.? Were there Christians in Herculaneum? The apparent imprint of a cross on a wall has been hotly debated as being evidence of Christian worshipers in the Town of Hercules.

The imprint is in a small upstairs room that may have been a chapel. The room has no windows and only one door. In the center of one wall is a square white plaster panel with a mark that looks as if it were left when a cross was hastily ripped away. Most scholars now agree that this is in fact the mark of a cross, not the mark of an oddly shaped shelf. The white plaster panel is set above a wooden cabinet, which has an angled shelf at the bottom, perhaps for kneeling. The room appears to have been a place for worship. A terra-cotta jug, a plate, a bowl, a pot with a handle, and a lamp were the only other objects found in the room.

The Apostle Paul landed at a nearby town on the Bay of Naples in A.D. 61, on his way to Rome. It is possible that after

Paul's visit a small group of Christians began meeting to worship in the small upstairs room at Herculaneum.

Roman acceptance of foreign or new religions did not extend to those faiths that were seen as a threat to the Roman way of life. Christians refused to worship any of the Roman gods—including the deified emperors. To Rome's rulers, a religion like that was dangerous because it would offend the gods and would undermine the emperor's authority.

If people in Herculaneum were practicing Christianity, they may have done so secretly. That would explain why a room with a cross would be located in a secluded spot in the house. The true importance of the cross hastily ripped from the wall is historical. It shows that as early as A.D. 79 the cross had become a Christian symbol.

The modern excavations of Herculaneum revealed many extraordinary things, of which the room with the cross was not the least. But many more wonderful things remain embedded in the hardened pyroclastic flow. They await a new generation of archaeologists with new scientific tools, adequate funds, and new enthusiasm.

6

THE DEAD TELL THEIR STORIES

A spectacular find of human skeletons provides much more than a horrible display of death. Those "old bones" speak volumes about the details of people's lives.

For a long time it was thought that almost all of Herculaneum's residents had escaped when Vesuvius exploded. Only a few skeletons of actual victims had been found: five people on a shelf in the Forum Baths, a man in an upstairs room, two people lifted 25 feet above the rooftops by the pyroclastic flow, a baby in a crib, a man in a locked room at the Shrine of the Augustales, and an adolescent boy in the gem-cutter's shop.

At Pompeii, the story was different, and it appeared as if more people had died there than at Herculaneum. Some of the citizens of Pompeii did not or could not rush to safety. They were the ones who were felled by the hot, dense mixture of fine ash and gases contained in the deadly glowing avalanche. As they died in spasms, their bodies were covered by a heavy fall of ash. With time, their flesh and bones decomposed, leaving hollow spaces in the solidified ash. Giuseppe Fiorelli, director of excavations in the 1860s, discovered that when plaster of Paris was poured into these spaces, the last dying moments of each

Dr. Bisel named her the Ring Lady, and deduced from her skeleton that she was a forty-five-year-old woman with "buck" teeth who probably was not good-looking. She was certainly wealthy, though. In addition to the two gold rings set with gems that she wore on her left hand, she was carrying heavy gold bracelets, gold earrings, and gold coins in a pouch at her side.

Along what was once Herculaneum's beach and marina, the town's ancient walls have archways leading to boat storage chambers. In this photo, one of the openings has been partially excavated. Townspeople must have sought refuge from Vesuvius in the dark, cavelike rooms—but to no avail. The skeletons of hundreds of victims are entombed here, preserved by the wet volcanic material that killed them 1,900 years ago.

person could be re-created. The life-size plaster casts are dramatic and frightening to see.

Because the Romans practiced cremation, very few Roman skeletons had ever been found by archaeologists. For this reason, little had been known about the Romans physically: about their average height, their teeth, their nutrition, their diseases. By looking at paintings and portrait statues from Roman times, we know what wealthy people looked like. But of the "man in the street" almost no information has come down to us. In fact, we probably know more about the bodies of very early Neolithic people, ancient Egyptians, and ancient Greeks than about ancient Romans.

All that changed in 1980. The scene was the marina at Herculaneum, where the ancient beach lies 13 feet below current sea level. Groundwater tables are so high that the Suburban Baths, for example, would be partially submerged if water were not pumped out day and night. To protect the site, director of excavations Giuseppe Maggi ordered that a new drainage ditch be dug across the ancient marina. While digging the trench, workers made an unexpected discovery. Their pneumatic drill and spades turned up portions of a skeleton. With care, an entire skeleton was uncovered. Then three more. The archaeologists at Herculaneum became very excited. They felt that they were on the verge of a major find—a find that would make history.

They were right. In 1982, the skeletal remains of hundreds of the volcano's victims were found in the boat chambers along the marina. It was clear that many, many citizens of Herculaneum had not escaped when Vesuvius erupted. Then came other surprises: a Roman boat 30 feet in length, keel up. A small horse—too small to carry a person. A man with an oar beside him (he had drowned and been cast up on the beach). And, most astonishing of all, a soldier slammed face down, along with his sword belt and sword.

A specialized scientist was needed to examine the skeletons and analyze the bones. So, when the size of the find and its importance became clear, the Italians appealed to the National Geographic Society in Washington, D.C., for help. The Society asked Dr. Sara C. Bisel, a physical anthropologist-archaeologist whose specialty was bones, to go to Herculaneum. She had been working in Greece and was close at hand. Amazed by what she heard, Dr. Bisel flew at once to Italy.

After her first look at the skeletons, Dr. Bisel said, "This is definitely a very major find—the first Roman population we have ever had to study. It's the first time we've known what ancient Romans really looked like."

Dr. Bisel set up a laboratory and began a program to study the skeletons. Each bone had to be washed, dried, measured, and dipped in a chemical to preserve it. Without the dip, exposure to air would have caused the bones to crumble like chalk. Then came the jigsaw puzzle of putting the bones back together again. Once the bones were reassembled, deductions could be made about each person's life. Dr. Bisel was to become a kind of scientific Sherlock Holmes. Very few secrets of the dead victims could be kept from her.

After the project was under way, Dr. Bisel chose individual skeletons for special attention. To begin, she picked the first skeleton she had seen: a woman who had been hurled off the town wall to the beach below. Her bones had been shattered by the fall. Her skull and pelvis had been crushed. One leg had been jammed into her neck. Dr. Bisel discovered that she was about forty-eight years old, stood 5 feet 1 inch tall, and had protruding "buck" teeth. She had high levels of lead in her bones.

Today we know that lead is a poison, but Romans were not aware of that. Many people were exposed to lead on a daily basis. It was used in pottery glazes, in paints, even in makeup. In wineries, grapes were boiled down in lead pots to make a syrup used to sweeten cheap wine. If she had worked in a winery (either as a slave or as a wage-earner) or if she had been a heavy drinker, that would account for lead buildup in her bones. But Vesuvius accomplished what dangerous levels of lead had not: her death.

The skeleton of another woman lay close by. She had not been blown off the town walls, but was felled on the beach. She came to be known as the Ring Lady because of her expensive jewelry. She wore two gold rings set with precious stones, and she carried with her two gold earrings and two heavy gold bracelets with matching snakes' heads. (In 1990, this valuable jewelry was stolen from the Herculaneum storehouse; fortunately, it was later recovered.)

The Ring Lady was about forty-five years old, well-fed, and taller than average. Her teeth were in excellent condition. It is clear that she was a wealthy woman. Her jewelry was a treasured possession that she clung to even as her world collapsed around her.

Another female skeleton was called by Dr. Bisel the Pretty Lady. She was about thirty-five years old. Dr. Bisel said that "she had a lovely face of rare proportion, perfect teeth, and a dainty nose." She was 5 feet tall; her bones were slender and her arms well exercised.

The remains of a pregnant twenty-five-year-old were also unearthed. We know that she was blond because a patch of hair still clung to her skull. The term of the unborn baby was about seven months. Its bones were as fragile as eggshells.

Another pregnant woman examined by Dr. Bisel was only sixteen years old. The Romans considered a girl of thirteen and a boy of fourteen old enough for marriage. So quite possibly she and her husband had rushed to the beach together.

One of the saddest finds was a group of twelve skeletons, probably a family and their slaves: three men, four women (including one teenager), four children, and a baby. Dr. Bisel explained that it is very difficult to determine the sex of a child from a skeleton. But of the children, ages three, five,

> **ASSEMBLING THE PAST**

By comparing different types of ancient evidence, we can try to imagine what the very real people who lived out their lives along the Bay of Naples 2,000 years ago might have looked like.

Plaster cast.

In the late 1800s, Giuseppe Fiorelli devised a technique for making plaster casts using the impressions of victims' bodies left in the hardened volcanic rock. The cast shown here vividly re-creates the clothing and proportions of a victim from Pompeii.

To an expert like Sara Bisel, a woman's

Skeletal remains.

bones hold clues to her appearance and life-style.

Did the person whose skull is shown here look anything like the lovely Roman woman depicted in a wall painting from the Town of Hercules?

Ancient artwork.

nine, and ten, one was certainly a girl: the three-year-old was wearing gold-and-pearl earrings. To this day, little girls in southern Italy always wear earrings. The five-year-old was probably a boy. Surprisingly, he had cavities in his teeth and an abscess. Romans did not use sugar, so cavities were rare. If he had been bothered by a toothache, he must have soon forgotten it on that frightening night.

In this group, two skeletons were movingly intertwined. A fourteen-year-old girl had died clasping a baby in her arms. The baby was wearing little bells and a pin shaped like a cupid. Dr. Bisel saw at once, from the teenager's pelvis, that she was not yet old enough to bear a child. Then whose baby was she clutching so protectively? The girl's bones—then 1,903 years old—told Dr. Bisel a story of hardship and sacrifice. From the shape of her skull, Dr. Bisel thought that the girl had been pretty. But apparently her life had not been easy. Her teeth showed that as an infant she had starved or been very sick. Only a week or two before the eruption, two of her teeth had been pulled, probably without much anesthetic. Her bones showed that she had done work, especially lifting, that was unhealthily strenuous. It is likely that this young girl was the family's nursemaid, and she was almost certainly a slave. Yet in death she clung to the baby as if it were her own. She must have been a loving, caring person and a good nursemaid.

Skeletons of many more children and youths were found. Among them was a sixteen-year-old boy who evidently was a fisherman. Probably, like boy-fishermen today in Italy, he worked with his father. Fishermen then, as now, rowed standing up. The boy's arms and upper body showed muscular strength developed since childhood. His teeth were worn from holding cords in his mouth while fixing nets. Tools for mending, and the nets themselves, were found in Herculaneum. The tools were identical with those used today—except that the boy's tools were made of bronze and today's tools are plastic.

A man found with an oar might also have been a fisherman. Marks on the bones of his upper arms, Dr. Bisel said, showed that he had done heavy manual labor. That labor might have been rowing, or carrying stones or bricks on his shoulders in construction work. Perhaps he was a slave. He was about forty-five years old—elderly by Roman standards—and his life had been hard. "He did not have good food, good treat-ment, good anything," Dr. Bisel said. At first it was thought he might have been the helmsman of the nearby boat. Rudders had not yet been invented, so Romans used steering oars instead. But studies of the levels of volcanic flow revealed that the body had not been cast ashore at the same time as the boat. Although they don't necessarily go together, both give a vivid picture of the wild conditions on the beach that night.

The star of all the skeletons proved to be the Soldier. His body was outstretched, his hands grasping the earth. He had fallen forward, as if knocked from behind by a single great blow. He was wearing his sword belt and sword, and also a belt for a dagger. The dagger was missing. In his money belt he carried three gold coins and some silver. One of the coins bore the head of the fat-necked Emperor Nero. On his back was a carpenter's kit with a hammer, an adze (for cutting wood), a hook, and two chisels. Roman soldiers were required to have a trade; when not off fighting wars, they were often assigned to building projects. The Soldier may have been a marine carpenter. He had kept a cool head, and with his sword, money, and tools he was well prepared to ride out an emergency.

The Soldier was slammed face down on the beach. When he was unearthed, his sword was along his right side and his tool kit was on top of him. This is the only skeleton ever found of a Roman soldier.

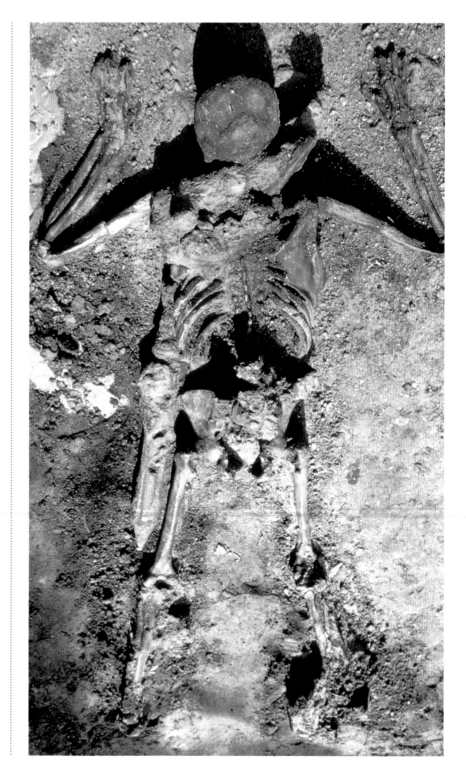

"Ride out" seems to be exactly the right phrase, because this Roman soldier apparently was a cavalryman. Dr. Bisel was fascinated by his physical characteristics. To begin with, he was taller than average: his height was more than 5 feet 8 inches. His thigh bones showed evidence of the strong muscles needed for riding a horse bareback (Romans did not use saddles). The bones of his right arm and shoulder showed the muscular buildup needed for slashing and thrusting with a sword and for tossing the javelin. His left thigh recorded where a wound had healed without leaving permanent damage. He was about thirty-seven years old and had always eaten well. Even so, six of his teeth were missing, including three in front. The three front teeth had been knocked out when he was younger, per-haps in a battle. "He was a pretty tough character," Dr. Bisel said, "[but] not at all good-looking. He lost those teeth, and his nose was really quite large. But he was well-off." He is the only Roman soldier whose remains have come down to us after almost 2,000 years. He aroused such interest that he was taken to Washington, D.C., for exhibition by the National Geographic Society. Many people came to view his bones, his carpentry kit, and his sword.

By the time Dr. Bisel had examined 139 skeletons in detail, she felt she had a good cross-section of the Roman popu-lation. Young and old, male and female, poor and rich, enslaved and free were represented in her sample. Dr. Bisel found that the average height was about 5 feet 1 inch for women, 5 feet 5 inches for men. She was impressed at the amazingly good condition of their teeth. The skeletons showed little evidence of dental disease. They averaged only about three cavities each, and most teeth were a beautiful bright white. Herculaneans owed their good dental health to a well-balanced diet that

A small wooden coin box found on the beach once belonged to a Roman citizen.

An archaeologist carefully examines the hull of a 30-foot Roman boat, shown in the upside-down position in which it was found. The outside of the boat was badly charred by the eruption's intense heat and is very fragile. The well-preserved interior offers a wealth of information about ancient boat-building.

included seafood, a good source of fluoride. They had no refined sugar and used just a little honey for sweetening. They did not drink coffee or tea and, most importantly, did not smoke. They cleaned their teeth regularly by rubbing them with the brushy ends of sticks or twigs.

Despite Dr. Bisel's first shock at the levels of lead in the smashed woman's body, she found only one other—a man—with a high concentration. He might have been a plumber or someone who worked with lead utensils. Only six other people showed medium concentrations. All the rest had no more lead than did Greeks of the same period, and only slightly more than what had been found in prehistoric skeletons (from before the discovery of metal-working).

This evidence calls into question the theory that lead poisoning contributed to the fall of the Roman Empire. Some scholars have suggested that the lead pipes used for transporting water would have resulted in toxic levels being consumed. But before water reached those pipes, it had traveled from the mountains through stone aqueducts, and thus was high in calcium, which helps make strong teeth and strong bones. Calcium in the water supply coated the lead pipes with an inner lining. (This still happens in the city of Rome.) Very little lead could get through to the thirsty, then or now.

All of the skeletons examined by Dr. Bisel were carefully packed in yellow plastic boxes and are now stored in Herculaneum in a modern concrete and glass building originally designed as a small museum. Some skeletons will be studied by medical research scientists interested in the extent and history of diseases. Others are laid out for visitors to see.

The boat is also on display, wrapped in layers of plastic. Because it had been badly scorched and is very fragile, it has been handled with great care. It is a prized archaeological find, because—unlike most ancient wrecks—this boat's interior and upper hull are beautifully preserved. Its craftsmanship was of the highest quality. It was decorated with elegant carvings, and clearly was not a fishing boat. Perhaps it was one of the smaller craft in Admiral Pliny's fleet.

The many remaining unexplored boat chambers undoubtedly hold more bodies. As in Italian seaside towns and villages today, boats were stored in such chambers only in winter. So in Herculaneum the chambers would have been empty and could provide shelter. Some contained more skeletons than others. For example, one had twelve bodies, another twenty-six, still another forty. The forty were tangled in a heap. The twenty-six were laid out in a row, as if people in single file suddenly had been blown over.

As for the unexplored chambers, some people want to dig them out and study the skeletons bone by bone. Other people want to leave them in place, exposing some to view. Unfortunately, the bones will quickly disintegrate if left out in the open air. They can be preserved by removing, cleaning, and dipping. But efforts to preserve them in place have not been very successful.

Perhaps the best solution would be to open the boat chambers and then make careful photographic records before removing the bones. The dramatic photographs could be enlarged and placed on display. Scientists could go on with their studies, giving us more and more facts about the lives of ancient Romans.

The ferry boat shown in this wall painting from the Roman port of Ostia is about the same size as the boat found in Herculaneum. Workers can be seen carrying cargo on board and pouring grain into a large container.

7

HOW WEALTHY PEOPLE LIVED

The lavish houses of Herculaneum's important citizens were designed with beauty, comfort, and utility in mind.

Today we surprise the people of Herculaneum, so to speak, because we walk into their houses uninvited. So we learn the most about their lives. Nobody can put up a false front, tidying rooms normally in disorder or hiding the pictures and statuary. Everything is exactly as it was, including doodles on the walls.

On the southern edge of town, on top of the old, pre-Roman town wall, a row of houses faces the marina. Now the sea is far away from its former boundaries, driven back by the pyroclastic flows delivered by Vesuvius. But when these houses were built they overlooked the bay and took advantage of the sea breezes and the view. They were equipped with terraces, arcades, balconies, hanging gardens, fountains, arbors, statues.

The houses on the wall were much more colorful than houses today. Rows of columns were painted red, and roof tiles were a dark yellow terra-cotta. Mosaics glinted with blue and gold. They were luxurious and elegant houses, perfectly

The photo (opposite page) shows patrician houses built on top of the old town wall as they appear today. Their gardens, sun rooms, verandas, and open-air dining rooms took advantage of spectacular views of the marina and the Bay of Naples.

The drawing below conveys how the southern edge of these homes probably looked in A.D. 79. The House of the Mosaic Atrium is in the foreground.

The dramatic checkerboard-patterned floor of the House of the Mosaic Atrium was severely distorted by the Vesuvian flow. Even the large central basin buckled under the weight of volcanic deposits. Earth tremors probably contributed to the damage.

designed for hot summer days and the seashore. These houses belonged to a class of wealthy Romans known as patricians.

Looking up at the houses from where the ancient beach-front used to be, a visitor almost expects a figure in Roman dress to appear, wave, and call a friendly greeting. A steep incline leads up through the Marine Gate into the town. Entrances to the patrician houses face on various streets.

One of the best preserved is called the House of the Mosiac Atrium. (Excavators and archaeologists have given each dwelling a descriptive name based on some special feature.

Houses were not known by these names in ancient times.) Inside the doorway is an entrance hall (the fauces), with a small room on either side. The room on the right is a kitchen, the one on the left is where the doorkeeper and his dog stayed. Their job was to keep unwelcome visitors away. Our word "janitor" comes from the Latin name for the doorkeeper: *ianitor*.

The entrance hall leads to the atrium. Here the mosiac floor is a geometric design of large black and white rectangles. It was forced into wavy shapes by both earth tremors and the enormous pressure of heavy volcanic deposits. In the center of the atrium, under the opening in the roof, is a white marble basin for catching rainwater. This is the impluvium, and, like the floor, it has been forced out of shape. Off the far end of the atrium is a large reception room called the tablinum, where the head of the household met with visitors. The statuary that undoubtedly adorned these rooms is missing. It might have been swept away by the volcanic flow down the slope toward the sea, or, more probably, it was removed by the early tunnelers.

The owners took full advantage of the site by building what amounts to a second house on the very edge of the town wall. The two sections are connected. The architects were thinking about the climate. Then, as now, summer days were hot, with brilliant sunlight; winter days were sometimes rainy and overcast, sometimes clear but cold with a strong northeast wind (there was rarely ice or snow); spring and autumn days were cool, with bright sunlight. Enclosed walkways between the two sections of the house were the architects' answer.

A garden was laid out and walkways constructed on either side. The path that faced the cold east winds was brick enclosed, with small windows to let in light. The walkway on the opposite side was protected by large sheets of glass held in

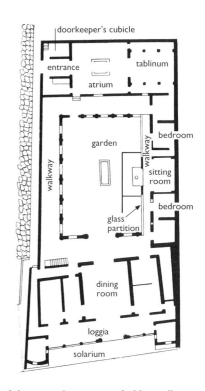

A large garden surrounded by walkways dominates the floor plan of the House of the Mosaic Atrium. The dining room, loggia, and solarium overlooked the sea.

In the 1930s, an ambitious restoration project brought the garden of the House of the Mosaic Atrium back to life. As seen in a photo from that time, a small fountain spurts in the marble pool, and authentic plantings re-create the feeling of relaxed elegance enjoyed by wealthy residents twenty centuries ago. Unfortunately, today this garden lies untended and overgrown.

place by narrow strips of wood. The original wood, though charred, is still there, but the glass was broken long ago.

In the 1930s, under the direction of archaeologist Amedeo Maiuri, workers restored the garden by replacing the weeds that had sprouted with the native plants of 2,000 years ago. Archaeologists used the imprints of roots remaining from ancient plants to guide them. The paths where peacocks once strutted were once again covered with gravel. A jet of water even splashed upward through its original lead pipe into a rectangular marble basin where goldfish swam. Regrettably, that ambitious restoration has not been maintained.

Behind the glass-enclosed walkway is a pleasant small sitting room overlooking the garden. The walls, decorated with two landscape paintings, are colored an azure blue. One painting, *The Punishment of Dirce*, shows a mythical woman who was tied to a bull as punishment for her own cruelty. The other painting, *Diana Bathing*, shows the goddess of the hunt at her bath. On either side of the sitting room are two bedrooms with red walls and stuccoed ceilings. In one is a round, three-legged table with each leg carved in the shape of a cat's head. On the table, a round loaf of bread was found. Both table and bread were charred during the eruption.

A lush and colorful garden scene celebrates the beauty of nature in this Herculaneum mural.

An imposing triclinium, or dining room, was built near the edge of the town wall, where diners would have a sweeping view of the sea. The furniture has disappeared, but the room probably had three couches in a U-shaped arrangement and a low table in the center. Here, the wealthy owner of this seaside home would impress his guests with lavish dinner parties. Up to three people would relax on each couch. Servants would bring food and watered-down wine to the table. In A.D. 79, both men and women ate while reclining on the couches. In earlier Roman times, however, the women sat at a table while the men reclined.

In such a house as this, the table would have been made of bronze, with a marble top. The couches would have been wood inlaid with silver or gold and mother-of-pearl, amber, or ivory. For extra comfort, dining couches sloped upward at one end. Sometimes the frame was curved in the form of a swan's neck. The cushions were of various colors and made of the finest soft materials. Dishes, knives, and spoons were probably silver. Romans did not use forks at the table; meat was cut in advance by a servant called the "scissor."

> **FOOD AND FEASTS**

Wealthy Romans enjoyed turning the late afternoon meal into a leisurely social occasion, with elaborate foods served in course after course. Musicians, dancers, poets, tumbling dwarfs, and other performers might entertain the guests. Banquets often lasted well into the evening hours. In this fresco from Pompeii, diners recline on couches in the typical Roman fashion. This must be toward the end of the meal—the table has been removed to make it easier for the slaves to assist over-stuffed guests.

Food and drink for lavish meals were prepared in small, dark kitchens like the one shown below, which was discovered with 2,000-year-old pots and pans sitting on top of the hearth. Slaves stoked the fire by shoveling red-hot charcoal through the large openings. While sauces simmered on the top, meat, fish, and fowl were roasted in the ovens.

A Roman dinner party.

The kitchen in a house in Herculaneum.

The room's wall decorations have not survived. Perhaps, as in other patrician dining rooms, they were soothing pastoral scenes or paintings of fish or game. Romans greatly enjoyed good food and liked everything about dining to be agreeable.

Outside the dining room, facing south for warmth, is a covered arcade called a loggia. Just beyond is a small uncovered terrace or sun deck for sunbathing. The Romans called it the solarium. At either end of the loggia is a small shaded room. These little rooms were intended to catch both the sea breezes and the view. They were pleasant spots for napping during the heat of the day.

Objects found in the House of the Mosaic Atrium are prized by archaeologists and historians, even though their original owners probably never gave some of them a second thought as they went about their day-to-day business. For a time they were displayed in various rooms of the house, but they have since been either stolen or transferred to museum collections. They range from the luxurious to the mundane: a kitchen colander with holes pierced in a beautiful design, bronze bowls and glassware, a hatchet, decorations for a horse bridle, a wax tablet (a hinged, wax-covered wooden board for writing on), ladles for soup, bells, oil lamps, door handles made of bronze, a statuette of Venus, a fishhook, bronze candlesticks, perfume flasks, a bowlful of dates, and an intricately decorated lead water tank.

In the house next door, cooking utensils were found hanging above the kitchen stove. In another house, a wooden cradle still held the bones of a tiny baby. Many fine pieces of sculpture were discovered, including the *Drunken Hercules*, which pokes fun at the hero-god. On the wall in the latrine a famous graffito was signed by a doctor who said he was the

Household items discovered in Herculaneum show the care and craftsmanship lavished by Romans even on everyday objects. For example, a bronze kitchen colander displays an elaborate geometric design. The bronze drawer pull embellished with a pair of hands and the terra-cotta vase with a "face" both convey a touch of whimsy.

physician of Emperor Titus. The writer announced that he was extremely pleased with his bowel movement!

In 1938, one of the most important of the patrician houses was uncovered. It is called the House of the Bicentenary because it was discovered exactly 200 years after the beginning of organized exploration of Herculaneum. It was in this house that the room with a cross was found, and also the records of a lawsuit concerning a young girl named Justa. Justa's story is told in detail in Chapter 9.

Only a few people could afford the expensive houses along the wall above the sea. The rest of the patricians lived in less imposing houses on ordinary streets. And as bad times came—especially after the punishing earthquake that struck in A.D. 62—some newly pinched owners tended to become land-lords in order to make ends meet. By splitting up their houses into apartments and shops, they could collect rent. So, although they may have been upper-class citizens, not all Roman patricians were rich.

A wooden cradle contains the fragile bones of a baby, just as they were found in a patrician house. Why the baby was left behind is one of Herculaneum's unsolved mysteries.

This soaring, light-filled room is the atrium of one of the oldest houses in Herculaneum, the Samnite House. It was built at least 300 years before Vesuvius exploded. Originally, the second story consisted of an open balcony (or loggia) ringed by columns. Later on, the owners walled up sections between the columns to create an upstairs rental apartment.

Part of the history of "poor" patricians can be read in the Samnite House, built at least 300 years before the eruption. (Samnites controlled the Bay of Naples region from about 400 B.C. until their defeat by the Romans in 290 B.C.) When the house was new it had space—a courtyard, an upstairs loggia, a garden, many rooms. But in Roman times the house was changed. The open-air loggia was bricked in. A new doorway was added, giving access by steep stairs to a tiny apartment for rent. The courtyard and garden were sold, leaving the owners only what remained of the ground floor. The house had fallen on hard times.

Today a small painting depicting a mythological subject remains. It is called *The Rape of Europa* and shows Zeus, transformed into a powerful white bull, carrying away the princess Europa. The house contained a broken statuette of Venus putting on her sandals, fragments of wooden table legs carved in the form of dogs' feet, and a bowl of cookies.

On a wall in the Samnite House is a name scratched in Oscan letters: *SPUNES LOPI*. Oscan was the language spoken by the Samnites. Latin did not become the official language of the Town of Hercules until 89 B.C., 168 years before the town's destruction. Historians are intrigued by the evidence of the Oscan language in the Samnite House. Was *SPUNES LOPI* written when the house was new—that is, before Latin was imposed? Or did the house remain in the hands of an Oscan-speaking Samnite family up until Vesuvius struck? Another wall-writing is not in Oscan but in Latin. Its English translation is: "Let love burn here!" So perhaps both the Latin and the Oscan languages were spoken by the owners.

The front of the "poor" patrician House of the Wooden Partition is preserved better than any other house in Herculaneum or Pompeii. With its little windows on the street side, it looks just like some present-day houses in certain parts of Rome. The main difference is that the wooden roof beams of the Herculaneum house are charred.

This is a big house. It runs the entire length of the block, with entrances on separate streets. It is a typical noble house of pre-Roman days. The rooms have high ceilings and are decorated from top to bottom. But the most striking feature, the one that gives the house its name, is the large wooden partition that can be closed to separate the two largest rooms.

The partition originally was composed of three hand-

somely paneled double doors. The central section was destroyed in the 1700s by careless Spanish tunnelers, who bored straight through the wood. The doors' reconstruction in their original place is a triumph. The 2,000-year-old wood swings on 2,000-year-old hinges. The bronze handles are just as before. Bronze supports designed to look like ship ornaments still hold lamps. The ancient carpenters and woodworkers, though lacking power tools, clearly would need no lessons from us today.

Lifelike depictions of flowers, shrubs, and ducks are painted on the garden walls. Inside the house, someone has scribbled an angry complaint on the wall of one room: "Mouse

The House of the Wooden Partition has large wooden panels that swing together to close off the atrium and separate it from the rest of the house. In the 1700s, Spanish tunnelers destroyed the central section of the partition, but the double doors that remain are beautifully preserved.

> **CLASSES OF ROMAN SOCIETY**

At the time of Vesuvius's eruption, Roman citizens and noncitizens were broken up into various groups or classes.

PATRICIANS were privileged, upper-class citizens. Patrician men had political power and held important government, military, and religious offices. Originally, patricians were very wealthy, but in later years of the Empire some families fell on hard times.

PLEBEIANS, or plebs, were ordinary working-class citizens—laborers, craftsmen, shopkeepers, and farmers. Men of this class could vote and eventually became an important part of the Roman senate.

SLAVES made up a large part of the population and were essential to the economic functioning of Roman society. They performed skilled and unskilled jobs, working as laborers, household servants, craftsmen, teachers, and doctors. Under Roman law, slaves had no rights whatsoever. Although some were treated kindly by their masters, many led lives of misery. The system allowed slaves to be freed, eventually by no more than a spoken word.

FREEDMEN and FREEDWOMEN were former slaves who had bought or were granted liberty. Many became Roman citizens. Most retained social and financial ties to their former masters.

is a low-life," says the writer. During later excavations, many small objects were found in this house. The pulls for a chest of drawers resemble some still made today. Other familiar-looking household items from the House of the Wooden Partition are strap hinges, pincers, bowls, ladles, glass jars, belt buckles, bells, a lock and key, beads, a hatchet-hammer, a straw broom, blue chalk, chick-peas, perfume flasks. A set of black-and-white playing pieces for a board game (perhaps backgammon) are only a little different from ours, and a pair of dice are exactly the same. Sandals for horse hooves (to prevent slipping on stone) are woven of cord, just like some beach sandals today.

The most astonishing object of all is an ordinary piece of bread. It was broken from a loaf by a person who was just beginning lunch when Vesuvius exploded. Now its charred remains are fused to a portion of the tablecloth.

Although they were not patricians, another prosperous group lived in Herculaneum: successful merchants and commercial people. For convenience, we can call them the middle class, even though that concept was not known back then. Their houses all have the same problem: lack of space. Big houses cost too much for middle-class purses. To compensate, some merchants decorated their houses just as lavishly as upper-class citizens did, with wall paintings, mosaics, statues. The results were often magnificent. Sometimes, though, middle-class homeowners could not afford quality artists or craftsmen and decorations were crudely made.

It is from the middle-class houses in Herculaneum that most of our knowledge of Roman wooden furniture has come. Roman houses, like Greek houses, were sparsely furnished, but each piece of furniture tends to be of very high quality. Thanks to the solidified volcanic matter, we can actually see the same furniture used by the ancient inhabitants of Herculaneum. Most of the wood is charred, and the finish and upholstery have disappeared. All the same, it is easy to imagine the appearance of the original, because the whole structure is there before our eyes.

The middle-class House of the Wooden Shrine was named for a well-preserved household item: the combination cupboard and shrine shown in Chapter 5. The shrine, with its double function, indicates Roman thriftiness. The top is a miniature temple for honoring the home's protecting spirits, the lares and penates. Statuettes of these "household gods" were kept in the shrine, behind double doors. On the bottom, closed shelves held perfume flasks, buttons, pincers, a strigil (for scraping off oil and sweat at the baths), dice, a glass fruit bowl, a dish of garlic, and a statuette of Mercury.

In another room is a good example of the small round table that early Americans used to call a "candle stand." When unearthed, it held a woven straw basket and a cup of pine nuts. Upstairs, a large number of wax tablets were found under a bed. Romans used these wax-coated wooden boards for schoolwork, household records, business transactions, and legal accounts. Words on the wax tablets were scratched with a sharp tool called a stylus. (Books and permanent documents were written with pen and ink on papyrus, a paperlike material made from Egyptian reeds.)

The wax tablets found in the House of the Wooden Shrine were not legible, but archaeologists were able to figure out who the owner was on the basis of another clue. They found the personal seal—a stamp for imprinting a name on hot

The bronze legs of this small folding stool were fashioned in the shape of birds' beaks. Greeks and Romans did not like to clutter their houses with unnecessary furnishings, so folding stools were often used. The wood and fabric of this stool have been restored.

The sundial from a Herculaneum garden divides the day into twelve hours from dawn to sunset. Thus, summer hours were longer than winter hours.

Excavators unearthed this wonderfully decorated bronze gladiator's helmet in Herculaneum, although scholars don't know if it was ever actually worn there.

wax—of the house's owner. His name was Lucius Autronius Euthymius.

The house next door has a list of gladiators, and in another house a gladiator's helmet was discovered. Although it is not known whether the Town of Hercules had an arena or amphitheater for these violent spectator sports, an arena did exist in neighboring Pompeii. The list and helmet are interesting finds in a Greek-Roman town. Greeks generally did not favor the type of public spectacle in which gladiators fought other gladiators or wild beasts to the death before large crowds. (The Romans acquired this type of spectacle from the Etruscans.)

Bedroom furniture was especially well preserved in all houses, rich and poor. There were a few double beds, but most were single. In upper-class houses, beds were more elaborate. Often their legs had been shaped by lathes and ornamented with bronze or silver. Most beds had wooden panels at the head and on one side, to protect the sleeper from the damp stone walls of the room. Mattresses probably were made of fine-combed wool, or, in summer, a sweet-smelling grass. Usually, a square or rectangular arrangement of slats supported the mattress, but sometimes ropes were slung between the frames for that purpose.

The House of Neptune is richly decorated and has a large cereal and wine shop attached to it. It is one of the most interesting of all Herculaneum's middle-class houses because it is not intact. The wall facing the street was either shaken down or pushed out by the pyroclastic flow. It is sheared off as if Vesuvius had planned to place the contents of the house on display, like merchandise in department store windows. On an upper floor, visible from the street, a bedroom contained a wooden bed, bronze candelabrum, and marble table—all perfectly preserved.

In Roman times, this couch from the House of the Charred Furniture was upholstered and had many soft cushions; now only the frame remains. The small wooden table standing nearby was found with the owner's noonday meal still upon it. (For safety, the table and lunch dishes have since been enclosed in a modern glass display case.)

To the right, the latrine is laid open. A pipe going from the seat all the way down to the sewer is clearly visible.

The house was given its name because of an elaborate mosaic showing the god of the sea, Neptune, with his wife, Salacia, the goddess of salt water. (Their Greek names are Poseidon and Amphitrite.) In the mosaic, Neptune is naked and his wife is partially draped. They are done in glittering gold, below a huge conch shell. It is a work of art fit for a palace—but it adorns a small, open-air room of a wealthy small-town merchant. The house's owner had impeccable taste and hired skilled artisans. In the room where Neptune and Salacia are displayed, the owner made up for the lack of a garden by commissioning many-colored mosaics of floral designs. No living flowers could equal their brilliance. Built-in fountains added a soothing note to leisurely summer dinners.

Within the house, all of the walls are skillfully painted with beautiful frescoes. In the entrance hall, a bust of Hercules

In the House of Neptune, the middle-class owner managed to compensate for the absence of a garden. He covered the walls of this small open-air room with brilliant, many-colored mosaics and built fountains in niches along the back wall. The house is named for the beautiful mosaic on the right-hand side of the photograph, which depicts the sea-god, Neptune, and his wife, Salacia. In the summer, it must have been a delightful spot to enjoy a meal, with the blue sky above, sea breezes cooling the air, and the sound of water playfully splashing nearby.

and a statuette of Jupiter welcome visitors. Fine decorations did not deter people from scribbling messages on walls throughout the house: here, a list of wine deliveries with their dates; there, a list of spelling words to be learned by a schoolboy.

One of the doors in the house leads to the back entrance of the best-preserved and most completely equipped shop discovered in Herculaneum or Pompeii. The merchant did a brisk business selling cereal, wine, and olive oil, as well as hot soup and other cooked foods. Wooden scaffolds holding wine containers called amphorae and wooden supports for shelves were found intact. The cross-hatched wooden grill separating a part of the shop was unbroken. A coiled rope hung on a pin and a lamp hung from a hook. Charcoal in the stove was prepared for

In the shop attached to the House of Neptune—the most complete of its type ever discovered—you can see storage containers and serving bowls, as well as wooden shelves and scaffolding. Charred fava beans and chick-peas, still popular in modern Italy, were found in some of the terra-cotta jars.

kindling a fire. Large containers called dolia were full of cereals, and beans and chick-peas were for sale out on the counter.

We can only imagine with what regret the owner fled from this house and shop. How upset he must have been when his front wall collapsed! Perhaps he remembered that Neptune was not only god of the sea, but earth-shaker too. No matter how well a man lived, he was helpless before the gigantic uncontrolled forces of nature.

8

HOW WORKING PEOPLE LIVED

In the Town of Hercules, well-preserved apartments, workshops, and stores call attention to the ordinary business of day-to-day life.

Roman wealth was not produced by magic, but by hard-working Roman citizens and slaves. The houses, shops, and workshops of merchants and craftsmen in Herculaneum are easy to recognize. Working people were called "plebs"—short for plebeians (as opposed to patricians).

Merchants often lived in small houses that were connected with or close to their shops. Craftsmen often lived in cramped quarters to the rear of their workshops. Sometimes space was used for both working and selling. As for slaves, they were given the smallest rooms, or those near the kitchen. Housing patterns in Herculaneum were changing. Workers had moved to the town after the A.D. 62 earthquake to help rebuild and repair damaged structures. They needed places to live, but what would an elegant seaside resort town have to offer? Two unusual buildings uncovered in the town are just what would be needed to house a growing plebian population.

A man sells round Roman loaves of bread to his customers, one of whom is a young boy. This painting is from the reception room of a baker's house in Pompeii.

One was a true apartment house where many low-income families lived. The other was a cheaply constructed two-family dwelling. These two structures are important in the history of city construction, now called urban design. The Roman apartment building is the direct ancestor of modern multiple-housing units. The two-family dwelling is the only known complete example of a cheap, rapid-construction Roman house. The details of how to construct such a building were written down by the architect Vitruvius as early as 16 B.C.

The apartment house was big and impressive. It was over 265 feet wide and was at least four stories high. An unknown number of additional upper stories were destroyed in the eruption. (Five- and six-story apartment houses built entirely of brick or stone and wood were common in the city of Rome.) Most city people lived in apartment houses. The structures probably looked very much like apartment blocks in any modern city, except that in comparison the ancient apartments were more lavishly decorated.

The ground floor of the Herculaneum apartment building was divided into shops. Upper floors were reached by at least two different stairways. A large vaulted sewer has been explored. It is so big that it would have served many apartment units. It is easy to imagine wash day at the apartment houses, with clothing hanging from the balconies. Baskets would have been lowered down on cords from upper windows for small packages, just as they are today in Naples. Neapolitan children love to play games and tricks with these baskets.

The two-family house, in contrast to the massive apartment building, is as fragile as a bird cage. Strangely, it survived in far better shape than the apartment house. It stands next door to the patrician House of the Wooden Partition, and there could hardly be a greater contrast. The tenants who lived in the two-family house were undoubtedly poor plebians, while the people in the House of the Wooden Partition must have been wealthy upper-class Romans. You wonder whether the children of these two houses were allowed to play together. Normally, adult Romans of all classes rubbed shoulders, so perhaps the children did too.

This little structure is called the Trellis House. It is nothing more than a wooden skeleton of square frames. Each square is filled with stones and mortar crudely thrown together. Inside, partitions are constructed of flimsy strips of cane that are thinly plastered. An economical, fast method of construction was needed to meet the Roman population explosion, and this type of "trellis work" was the answer. One hundred years before Vesuvius erupted, the architect Vitruvius pointed out the disadvantages of trellis construction: lack of permanence, dampness, danger of fire. He would be astonished to learn that one such house has survived for 2,000 years.

In the Trellis House, some of the original steps are part of the reconstructed wooden staircase. Upstairs bedrooms have retained their red wall paint. The wooden beds, the wooden clothes cabinet, the wooden cupboard with utensils and statuettes of the household gods—all remain in their places. So do the marble tables. Only mattresses, linen, and clothing are missing. But the original rope, slightly scorched, is still wound on the original windlass for the well. The house was not connected to the town aqueduct, so residents had to draw their own water from a private well.

The working people or small traders who lived here reclined at meals in the same way that patricians and rich merchants did. We know this because a still-intact dining couch

Along this Herculaneum street, rich and poor lived side by side. In the right foreground, the large building is the elegant House of the Wooden Partition, a patrician home. Next door, two plebeian families lived in the cheaply built Trellis House.

This rope from the Trellis House was found exactly as you see it here, neatly coiled on top of a wooden windlass. Occupants attached a bucket to the rope and dropped it down their well. Then they rotated the windlass so that the rope would wrap around it and hoist the heavy, water-filled bucket back up again.

was found here. However, unlike patricians and wealthy residents, who indulged in lavish banquets and sumptuous meals, poorer people in the Town of Hercules ate much more simply. Bread and a kind of wheat porridge were dietary staples, supplemented by seasonings, olives, grapes, perhaps a little honey. They ate meat only occasionally, but living near the sea meant that fish and seafood were available. Like many of the houses and apartments of ordinary working-class people, the Trellis House did not have a kitchen. Take-out food was available from snack bars all over town, and perhaps also from taverns.

The Trellis House also yielded a doll carved of wood and about half of a marble oscillum with a horse carved on it. The round oscillum was the size of a dinner platter. In Roman houses, several were hung from the ceilings of outdoor peristyles in such a way that they could spin, or oscillate, for a pleasing decorative effect. Before it was broken, this oscillum may have hung in a patrician house. Perhaps a child who lived in the Trellis House found it in a junk heap and brought it home as a trophy. Even broken, it would have been fun to spin.

One of the games played by Roman children and adults was similar to our backgammon. A set found in the Trellis House was identical with one found in the patrician house next door. The glassware discovered here is good, and thumbtacks are still sharp enough for a school desk. On one wall, someone wrote that his friend Bacileus still remains in the town of Puteoli. If the former tenants could return, they would find it easy to take up living in their house again.

Scattered among the patrician homes in Herculaneum are many small houses attached to shops. The shops and workshops vary greatly in size and equipment. All merchants were not equally successful; all craftsmen not equally in demand. It appears that competition was fierce among them. Similar shops can still be seen on the back streets of many Italian cities today.

The largest shop yet discovered in Herculaneum was a thermopolium, or snack bar, just across the street from the entrance to the sports area (the Palaestra). This was a fine location—imagine a popular restaurant near a modern stadium. The snack bar's counter is faced with irregular pieces of marble in a variety of colors. Eight large jars called dolia are embedded in the counter itself. We know from chemical analyses that they contained various cereals and vegetables. Another larger jar perhaps held olive oil. Other jugs and amphorae (terra-cotta containers with pointed bottoms) may have been used to store different oils and sauces. A stove behind the counter was used to keep a variety of foods simmering in clay casseroles over the charcoal fire. The food was probably eaten while standing or taken out by the customer.

A spare room in the shop was rented to a wine merchant. We know this because a large number of wine amphorae were found there. The merchant may have been one of those wine exporters whose amphorae were marked in the Oscan language. Skin divers have found such amphorae in sunken Roman ships.

The snack bars and wine shops had a standard arrangement, always similar to the shop described above. Many counter displays remain intact: walnuts, almonds, dates, figs. In addition, cheeses, raisins wrapped in lemon leaves, and delicious little cakes were sold. Hot drinks also were served. The Romans were very fond of mulled or spiced wines of

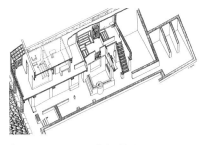

A cut-away view of the Trellis House shows the upstairs and downstairs; a different family lived on each floor. This plebeian building crams two apartments plus a store and workshops onto a narrow site. It represents a radical change from the large, airy spaces of a "typical" Roman atrium house.

A thermopolium like this one was the Roman version of a fast-food restaurant. Snacks and hot, ready-to-eat dishes were served from the terracotta storage jars, called dolia, which were recessed into the countertop. In Herculaneum, some homes and apartments did not have kitchens, and many people relied on snack bars and taverns for their meals.

many sorts, which were often sweetened with honey.

One of Herculaneum's snack bars has become especially well known because of its advertising. The phallic-god Priapus was boldly painted behind the counter for all passersby to see. The symbol of Priapus was believed to be effective against the evil eye, so any customer would be sure to be in luck. When it was unearthed, the counter still displayed walnuts that had been set out for sale. In the rear wall is a spy hole, through which the proprietor could keep an eye on the shop. Maybe he had trouble with small boys who snatched walnuts and ran away.

A few doors down the street is the shop of a cloth merchant. In this shop the modern excavators made an exceptional find: remnants of the ancient cloth itself. Now the material is displayed in a glass case, and the wavelike design is clearly visible.

Roman garments, with the exception of short tunics, used yards and yards of material. Quality had to be high so that clothing would be long-lasting. Cloth was made of wool or linen—silk was an expensive luxury. In earlier times, the main color had been white or near-white. Colored robes or tunics were worn only by foreigners or slaves. But later on, prosperous Roman women grew tired of the sameness of their clothes, so finer materials and a variety of colors were introduced. Later still, men began to wear color in their dinner clothes.

To meet the new demand, it was necessary for the dye industry to expand. Even a town as small as Herculaneum had several dye works. They are easy to recognize by the type of furnace used to heat the dye. The shops of clothes cleaners (sometimes called fullers) also have been found. Among other substances for cleaning, they used an alkaline clay now called "fullers' earth."

From another shop came one of the most important technological finds of antiquity: a cloth press. This device was used by fullers to "iron" cloth—to flatten it and smooth out wrinkles. The machine is 6 feet high and 2½ feet wide. It is constructed of hardwood, including its large worm screw. The most exciting fact about the cloth press is its appearance. It is very similar to the printing press invented almost 1,400 years later. Romans didn't realize it, but they could have used the press for printing with either wooden blocks or movable metal type. Actually, the basic principles were already understood: The bronze name seals used with sealing wax have letters that are raised from the surface and read in reverse, just like

A scale from a shop in the Town of Hercules still contains the merchandise that was being weighed at the moment Vesusius exploded. A mortar and pestle, left foreground, were used to grind materials into a fine powder.

We know what types of food were sold at certain snack bars because actual samples have survived intact. If Vesuvius had not struck, these walnuts would have been purchased and enjoyed by Herculaneum citizens.

This wooden press, for "ironing" cloth, was one of the most important finds of ancient technology. It is as tall as a man, with a central "worm" screw made of wood. Its resemblance to early printing presses is striking. Charred black by the heat of Vesuvius, it is now enclosed in a protective glass case.

the letters in a printing press. But somehow the concepts of the press and reverse-type were never connected. This now seems a tragedy, because if Romans had been able to print books inexpensively, that would have profoundly changed the Roman world.

Bread has been a dietary staple in Italy for thousands of years, and excavators have found several of the many bakeries that once thrived in Herculaneum. Today, Italian towns are still served by small neighborhood bakeries that open during the pre-dawn hours. In fact, they sell loaves of bread made in exactly the same shape as those sold centuries ago in Herculaneum. The bread is round with division marks so that the loaf can easily be broken into sections. It tastes much better than factory-made bread.

The largest bakery found in Herculaneum used a dome-shaped charcoal oven identical in shape with today's Neapolitan pizza ovens. Its iron door is tightly closed, and the lead water tank used for moistening the oven broom still stands nearby. Long wooden pallets for removing the loaves have disappeared. Historians believe that during the daytime this oven may have been used to bake dog biscuits, a Roman specialty for pets.

Here the grain was milled in the courtyard. Two mills were turned by a breed of tiny donkeys who walked continuously in a circle. They wore blindfolds so they wouldn't be distracted or startled. The animals' bones were found where they had died, in harness. Behind the bakery were both the stables and the baker's lodgings. The latter were handsome vaulted rooms with fine pavements and wall decorations.

The name of one baker in Herculaneum is known: Sextus Patulcus Felix. His seal was found in his shop. He specialized in cakes. We know this because twenty-five bronze baking

> ROMAN BAKERIES

Charred loaf of bread.

Bread was a principal element in the diet of people in the Town of Hercules. Because no one baked it at home, business thrived at various bakeries around town. At the bakery of Sextus Patulcus Felix (below right), excavators found the remains of large grain mills, an intact oven, and even an assortment of round baking pans hanging on the back wall—everything needed to go from grain to fresh-baked bread. The cone-shaped structures on the right side of the photograph are the bottom halves of stone mills for grinding flour. An intact mill (shown in a decorative scene from Ostia) had an hourglass-shaped upper portion, also made of heavy Vesuvian stone, that was turned by a tiny, blindfolded donkey. Grain was poured from above. As the animal walked in an endless circle, the movable top part rotated around the stationary bottom cone, and the wheat, barley, millet, or oat was ground into a fine flour.

Before dawn, Felix baked his bread and cakes in this dome-shaped oven.

A grain mill.

Two huge phallic good-luck symbols on its upper dome assured that the dough would rise. The finished product was a beautiful loaf of round

Felix's oven.

bread, notched to make it easier to break off chunks. Felix's oven and the charred bread shown here have survived nearly 2,000 years, yet they are almost identical to modern pizza ovens and round loaves of bread that can be found today throughout the Bay of Naples region.

The bakeshop of Sextus Patulcus Felix.

pans of various sizes were left hanging from a rack or in the oven. When he ran away, he also left stacks of money.

The flour mills were in the front of his shop. To one side, in a sooty two-story vaulted room, stood the round oven and its lofty chimney. The oven is perfectly preserved—you could cook in it today. Though this baker's name was "Lucky" (Felix), he took no chances with his luck. Over the oven door he placed two phallic good-luck charms, side by side, to make sure his cakes would rise during baking. And he placed two more charms in the dough room, where mixing bowls were found on a shelf. But as he fled, no doubt he cursed his luck.

Near the bakery was the luxury shop of a gem-cutter, or jeweler. We know a great deal about this shop. The owner had a considerable supply of gems that he displayed on a wide marble table. In the rear, he left behind a portrait bust with a damaged nose. He also left behind a child. An adolescent boy was found lying on an expensively decorated bed. The boy's bones indicate that he may have been paralyzed or ill. In the small room where he was found, a square inlaid wooden stool stood next to a small loom for weaving. In Roman times, weaving was "women's work," so it is likely that the boy had a companion, perhaps a slave or a freedwoman, who spent her time weaving while the boy rested. For the sick boy's lunch, chicken had been prepared, and a serving had been brought to his bedside. When the gem-cutter's house was excavated, the boy's bones were found in the bed, and equally well-preserved chicken bones were found in a nearby bowl.

How did it happen that the boy was abandoned? Were his father and mother absent? Was the woman old and unable to carry him away? Was he partially paralyzed, perhaps with polio, so that he himself could not leave the bed? Perhaps the

In a back room of the prosperous gem-cutter's shop, the skeleton of an adolescent boy was discovered. In this photograph, you can see the bones lying on an expensive couch richly decorated with inlaid wood. Nearby, a small, partially restored loom seems to await the weaver's return.

boy died before the family fled. Did his parents escape, or were they among the hundreds of victims found in the boat chambers? The boy in the gem-cutter's shop is another of Herculaneum's unresolved mysteries.

Many of the excavated shops in the Town of Hercules seem open and ready for business. It's easy to imagine that, at the ping of a coin, the proprietors will appear.

9

THE STORY OF JUSTA

Ancient legal records describe how a brave young
girl went to court to fight for her freedom.

In a small apartment next to the Christian "chapel" in the
House of the Bicentenary, eighteen wax writing tablets were
found unmelted. Also found was the seal of a man named
Helvius Eros, a Greek name. Amazingly, the tablets could still
be read. They are in three different handwritings and sometimes they are in a kind of legal shorthand. Of course, they are
in Latin, because they were official documents. They are the
records of a court case involving a teenage girl named Justa.

The wax tablets tell of a lawsuit brought by a middle-
aged woman named Calatoria Temidis in an effort to force
Justa, a free person, into slavery. Calatoria claimed that Justa
belonged to her. But Justa had spirit. She fought back.

The records tell almost the whole story, including the
names of witnesses, affidavits, verbal testimony, subpoenas,
and amounts of bail. Justa could never have dreamed that the
documents in her case would be read almost 2,000 years after
they were written. Not only were they read but they were

A view of the House of the Bicentenary, where Justa was born and raised.
In 1938, excavators discovered the
records of Justa's court case stored in
an upstairs room. (The open door to
the left is the entrance to the so-called
Christian chapel.)

Justa's court case was recorded on reusable wax tablets like these. A thin coating of wax was applied to the central recessed area of each wooden sheet. Romans wrote on the tablets by scratching the wax with the pointed end of a pencil-shaped tool called a stylus. Words could be erased by rubbing them with the blunt end of the stylus.

examined with care by learned professors of Roman law at famous universities.

The story began at about the time of the great earthquake of A.D. 62, when a baby girl was born in the household of a man named Gaius Petronius Stephanus and his wife, Calatoria Temidis (the plaintiff in the lawsuit). The baby's mother was a woman named Vitalis; her father was not acknowledged. Under Roman law, slaves were not permitted to marry, and children born to slaves automatically became slaves. Vitalis, the mother, had been a slave but was later freed.

The central issue was whether Justa had been born before or after her mother had been freed. Many records had been destroyed in the earthquake, so the case turned solely on verbal testimony. Witnesses were easy to buy and court procedures were slow and involved. The lawsuit seemed endless.

Apparently Petronius Stephanus had bought Vitalis as a wedding present for his wife, Calatoria. Vitalis was both intelligent and educated, so she was probably expensive. She must have deeply resented the white chalk on her feet at the auction block and the sales contract that sealed her fate. The contract was exactly the same as the one used for cattle.

Vitalis worked hard for her new mistress and gained the approval of her master. At about the time of the great earthquake, Vitalis was freed by her master. No reasons for this act were given in the court records. In earlier times, the act of freeing a slave had been a complex process. But by the first century, when the large majority of the population was composed of slaves, procedures had changed. In this case, it was necessary only for Gaius Petronius Stephanus to place his hands on Vitalis's head and say in the presence of witnesses, "I declare this woman no longer bound." Actually, Vitalis bought her own freedom, paying a 5 percent freedom tax.

Once free, Vitalis assumed her former master's name. She became Petronia Vitalis. And, though free, she remained in her master's household. There Justa was born. For a decade or more, all went well. In the master's words, according to court records, Justa "was brought up like a daughter." Indeed, Vitalis and Justa were even permitted to eat at the master's table—a privilege forbidden to slaves.

Like her mother, Justa was intelligent and educated. Very probably her tutor was the administrator–manager, an older freedman named Telesphorus. Once he had been Calatoria's tutor, and he had been helpful to Vitalis when she was brought into the household as a slave. Eventually, it became clear that Telesphorus and Vitalis had developed a close friendship.

After the birth of Calatoria's children, Justa became a nursemaid. Sometime afterward, friction arose between Vitalis and Calatoria, and Vitalis decided to leave the household. As a freedwoman, she could not be forced to stay. However,

Calatoria and Petronius Stephanus refused to let Justa go with her mother. So Vitalis departed, leaving her beloved daughter behind.

Vitalis had no intention of permanently abandoning Justa. She worked hard, day and night, accumulating both money and property. Then she returned in triumph to claim her daughter. Again, Calatoria and, especially, Petronius Stephanus refused to part with the girl. It is easy to imagine Vitalis's frustration and anger.

She planned a way to outwit her former master and mistress. She could not sue them; by law, a former slave could not bring a former master to court. But Justa, free, could sue for her own release to her mother. And Vitalis had acquired the funds to pay all legal fees. Petronius Stephanus proposed a compromise. Apparently, he did not wish to face the lawsuit. If Vitalis would pay him and his wife the cost of Justa's food, lodging, clothes, and schoolbooks for every year since her birth, then they would let her go. With the help of Telesphorus, an accord was reached. Though the cost was high, Vitalis paid for all past expenses. Lovingly, she took her daughter to her own household.

This happy state of affairs did not last long. Vitalis became ill, and died. In her will, she left all her property to her daughter. Justa was now alone, without a defender. Soon after Vitalis's death, Petronius Stephanus also died. It was then that Calatoria filed suit against Justa, claiming that Justa had been born before her mother was freed. As a slave, she belonged to Calatoria and was not eligible to inherit her mother's property. According to Roman law, if Justa were a slave, then everything bequeathed to her by Vitalis would belong to Calatoria—and Calatoria wanted to collect.

The case began with a hearing before a Herculaneum magistrate in the Basilica, which was the town's courthouse. Plaintiff (Calatoria) and defendant (Justa) stated their positions. The magistrate concluded that the case, which involved complex legal questions, should be heard before a judge, with witnesses, affidavits, and sworn testimony. He fixed bail for the appearance of both parties in the amount of 1,000 silver sesterces each. The pay of a Roman soldier for an entire year was 1,000 sesterces. For Calatoria this sum must have been trivial, but for Justa it would have been a burden. And Justa faced a serious threat: Penalties were very heavy for a slave who pretended to be free.

Eventually, the case came before a judge. It was the judge, not the lawyers (advocates), who had the authority to cross-examine witnesses. Once again the positions of both parties were stated, this time by advocates. No written records could be found to support the positions of either Calatoria or Justa. So witnesses were called. Affidavits were read aloud. Three of these are of special interest.

For Justa, a man named Quintus Talmudius Optatus testified that he was present when the discussions about Justa were going on with her mother. He heard Stephanus say, "Why are you so upset with us about the girl, when we are treating her as our own daughter?" Optatus knew, he said, that Justa was the daughter of Vitalis and free by birth.

For Calatoria, a witness appeared who could not read or write. His name was Marius Calatorius Marullus. His name shows that he, too, was connected with the Calatorius family. For his testimony, he seems to have been rewarded with his freedom. His testimony had to be read for him. His key statement was: "I knowed Calatoria Themis freed both the girl and myself. So I knowed that this here girl is a freedwoman of Calatoria Themis." To an objective observer reading the documents after 2,000 years, it seems likely that the man was lying.

Then a surprise witness testified for Justa:

I, Gaius Petronius Telesphorus, have written and sworn by the spirit of the sacred Emperor Vespasian Augustus and his sons that I know the girl Justa, defendant in this suit, was born free. She was the child of my fellow freedperson, Petronia Vitalis. It was I who arranged with Petronius Stephanus and Calatoria Temidis reimbursement for Justa's upbringing. It was I who helped restore her to her mother. From these facts I know that the girl Justa, object of suit, was born in freedom. This is the question at issue.

Telesphorus had dared to testify against his mistress, probably at serious cost to himself. We may imagine the astonishment in the courtroom, the shocked expression on Calatoria's face.

Despite this testimony, the judge refused to make a decision. His reasons are unclear. Perhaps Calatoria's relationship to the powerful Calatorius family had something to do with it. Perhaps the lack of documentary records made him uneasy. For whatever reason, he ruled that the case must be continued before a judge in the Forum of Augustus in Rome. He set the day and the time; then he set the amount of bail.

This action by the judge must have been very difficult for Justa to accept. The case was to drag on and on and on. At the time of the eruption of Vesuvius, no final decision had yet been made. We shall never know the outcome.

An interesting question remains: was Telesphorus the unnamed father of Justa? Certain phrases seem to hint at this. Otherwise, why would he have dared to testify against his mistress? The cost to him must have been considerable.

Telesphorus was a brave man, and Justa a brave girl. Let us hope that both escaped the rushing volcanic tide that buried the records of Justa's court battle. After all, Justa was named for the Latin word meaning justice: *justitia*.

WHERE JUSTA WAS TRIED: THE BASILICA

In the town's grand courthouse, beautiful paintings portray Hercules and other mythological heroes. Imposing statues of real people testify to the importance of the Balbus family in the community.

To the courthouse in Herculaneum, called the Basilica, came Justa in defense of her rights. The courtroom must have hummed with the whispers of lawyers and clients. The curious spectators must have stared at the young girl, and perhaps they shook their heads disapprovingly at greedy Calatoria. Little attention would have been paid to the impressive building itself.

In ancient Greece, the *basilikos* was the "King's house." The idea of kingliness in Rome was transferred to the courts of law, so the building where courts were located was known as the Basilica. It also contained business offices and usually followed a standard design: a rectangular hall rounded at one end (the apse), flanked on each side by an aisle with a row of columns. Sometimes galleries for spectators were erected at the sides. The judge wore a formal toga and sat in the apse, at a level above everyone else.

The Finding of Telephus, a wall-size fresco from the Basilica, shows Hercules recognizing his infant son, Telephus. The child had been abandoned by his mother in the forest and was nurtured by the doe shown suckling him. Mythological scenes were favorite Roman subjects for artistic expression.

An artist's view of what the ruins of Herculaneum's Basilica, or law court, might have looked like. The statues of Marcus Nonius Balbus and his son on horseback are just visible on either side of the long rectangular room. The Basilica was never fully excavated, so this watercolor is based on the reports of two Frenchmen who, in the 1700s, traveled through excavation tunnels to steal a glimpse of the still-buried structure. They had only the flickering light of hand-held torches to guide them.

Today the Basilica in Herculaneum is still buried, and the excavation tunnels leading to it are heaped with rubble and closed to any passage. They were refilled in the 1700s because the layer of volcanic matter is not as deep at this point, and the houses of Resina built on top were in danger of collapsing. However, it is still possible to penetrate a little way along one line of massive columns. Some are tilted on their bases like toppled bowling pins, but they remain locked in place by the solidified volcanic deposits.

The Basilica was not explored and measured carefully, but a rough plan does exist. Before the tunnels were closed, two curious French travelers walked through the buried courthouse with torches. Afterward they wrote a detailed description of their amazing experience. They reported that the Basilica is a large building, about 200 feet from front to back, with a long rectangular hall. The hall is divided by two side rows of columns into a central assembly space. Along the walls, niches held statues. At the rear was a huge figure of the Emperor Vespasian, who ruled Rome from A.D. 69 until just a few months before Vesuvius erupted. On either side of the apse were large semicircular niches with frescoes portraying mythological subjects.

These paintings eventually were removed and are now among the treasures of the National Archaeological Museum in Naples. One fresco shows the centaur Chiron, a creature that is half-man, half-horse, teaching a young hero named Achilles how to play the lyre. In classical mythology, Chiron was responsible for instructing Achilles in the "manly arts," the first of which was music.

Another fresco illustrates an incident from the life of the legendary founder of the town of Herculaneum. A sun-bronzed Hercules, shown from behind wearing only a flower garland and a quiver (for holding arrows), stands watching a naked little boy. The boy is being suckled by a doe, while the doe lovingly licks the child's leg. Hercules recognizes the boy as his own son, Telephus, who had been abandoned in a forest and was rescued by the doe.

The third fresco shows the Greek hero Theseus triumphant over the Minotaur, a monster with the body of a man and the head of a bull. Theseus has just stepped out of the labyrinth. Behind him the monster lies dead. The hero is nude, except for a purple cloak flung over his left arm. He carries his weapon, a large staff, in one hand. Naked youths kneel before him; in the background, a worshipful crowd looks on.

Who painted these lively, expressive scenes? Unfortunately, the frescoes are not signed. They are very skillfully executed and are considered among the best examples of ancient painting known to us. If a tiny town like Herculaneum could command such gifted artists for its courthouse, what of the great cities? Imagine having original masterpieces created for the courthouse in *your* town!

The Basilica was artistically remarkable for another reason: atop it was the largest bronze four-horse chariot and driver ever found from ancient times. These statues probably crowned the entrance. Unfortunately, they were swept away when the volcano erupted; fragments have been found in several different places. The patient work of reconstruction is like a jigsaw puzzle. One life-size horse is now complete and the head of another horse has been recovered. As each new piece appears, the beauty of the whole becomes more apparent.

The entrance to the Basilica was flanked by two larger-than-life-size marble statues of the Proconsul Marcus Nonius Balbus and his son, Balbus the Younger, on horseback. A proconsul was one of the most powerful of Roman officials, and Herculaneum was proud to be the hometown of such a person. Balbus was the Roman ruler of the island of Crete and portions of North Africa.

Inside the Basilica were the marble portraits of the entire Balbus family, all slightly larger than life. They were found still standing on their pedestals or fallen nearby. (All are now in the museum in Naples.) An inscription (now in the museum, too) states that, after the earthquake, Balbus used his own money to rebuild the Basilica. The letters are at least a foot large, chiseled in marble and painted red. A grateful town erected statues of the family and documented its patron's contributions.

The Balbus statues are fascinating because they are like a family photo album. In looking at them, it is tempting to speculate about the personality of each family member—and almost impossible not to wonder about their real-life relationships to one another. These were public portraits, however, and are meant to portray the family as it wished to be seen by the community. "Balbus" was not an old patrician name, so the family was not originally upper class. However, the Balbuses had been wealthy for several generations. Among the qualities conveyed in the statues are the subjects' sense of their own importance and prominence.

On their handsome marble horses, the proconsul and his son ride without saddles. They are dressed identically: each wears a thigh-length tunic, soft riding shoes, and chest armor; each has his sword in its scabbard and his cloak thrown over his left shoulder and left arm. The left hand of each statue holds the reins. On the third finger of each left hand is a large signet ring. The right hands are raised aloft in gestures of command. Both their faces are clean-shaven (and their legs may have been, too).

Although they are posed identically, father and son are distinguished from one another by the sculptor's attention to detail. The proconsul's hairline is receding, while the son's abundant hair is combed forward in the Roman fashion. The proconsul looks very much like an American business executive. He is self-assured in a formal, commanding sort of way. His son could easily pass for a high school or college student today.

The other members of the family are shown with vivid realism. The wife, Volasennia, is an average-looking Roman matron and seems a bit bored. Traces of reddish-blond paint

This life-size bronze horse was one of four harnessed to a great bronze chariot that is believed to have stood high atop the Basilica's entrance. The driver was a heroic figure, perhaps a Roman emperor. The entire group was swept away by the churning volcanic avalanche. Parts of the other horses, the chariot, and the driver continue to be discovered.

> **A ROMAN FAMILY ALBUM**

The Balbus family were important citizens and benefactors in the Town of Hercules. The head of the household, Proconsul Marcus Nonius Balbus, had paid to rebuild Herculaneum's town walls, gates, and Basilica after the great earthquake of A.D. 62. He was patron of the Theater and sponsored games in the Palaestra. Balbus family members are immortalized in larger-than-life-size marble statues that were publicly displayed in the Basilica. Townspeople had a daily reminder of the family's prominence.

Close-ups of each face invite us to speculate about character and personality. Modern viewers often remark that the proconsul looks like a successful, self-assured American businessman. His son seems a bit insecure—or is it rebellion we can read in his furrowed brow? The Balbus women range from intimidating to appealing. The depiction of the proconsul's mother, Viciria, demonstrates the sculptor's realism at its most candid. With her features frozen in an icy marble frown, Viciria does not look

like someone you would want to cross. Volasennia, the proconsul's wife, is stately and dignified. (Reddish paint stills clings to the statue's wavy hair.) The two daughters look youthful and kind. We do not know the girls' names for certain because the bases of their statues were not recovered from the Basilica, but they may have been called Nonia the Elder and Nonia the Younger. All of the Balbus statues are now in the National Archaeological Museum in Naples.

Proconsul Marcus Nonius Balbus
(Balbus the Elder).

Viciria, mother of Balbus the Elder.

Nonia the Elder.

Marcus Nonius Balbus
(Balbus the Younger).

Volasennia, wife of Balbus the Elder.

Nonia the Younger.

remain on her hair, indicating that she probably used a hair dye that was popular with Roman women at that time.

The two daughters may have been called Nonia the Younger and Nonia the Elder, from "Nonius," in accordance with old Roman custom. They look like proper, if somewhat plain, young ladies. Their hair has been parted in the middle and brushed back in close-fitting waves to a tight bun on the neck. Slight traces of red paint suggest that the older daughter may have colored her hair like her mother. The younger daughter is slim and has a shy, quiet expression.

In the powerful depiction of the grandmother, Viciria (mother of Balbus the Elder), a true masterpiece of Roman portrait art can be seen. This old-fashioned matron stares down at us from her pedestal, looking harsh, inflexible, dominating. Her stern, stony features are emphasized by a large nose. Her firm mouth and stubbornly set jaw make her look both tough and humorless. Her heavy body is wrapped in a cloak; a hood partly covers her head. Viciria's hair is parted in the middle and pulled severely back. Her strong right hand is raised almost to her chin. The Balbus household no doubt was well managed by grandmother Viciria, but it seems unlikely to have been a jolly place.

Written on a wall of the house that probably belonged to Balbus are two proverbs. They appear in tiny, regular letters:

WHO DOES NOT KNOW HOW TO DEFEND HIMSELF, DOES NOT KNOW HOW TO SURVIVE.

EVEN A SMALL DANGER BECOMES GREAT IF NEGLECTED.

It is easy to imagine a household ruled by the Balbus matriarch giving rise to such sentiments.

The courtyard of the house that almost certainly belonged to the Balbus family. The white disks hanging between the columns are marble oscilla, carved decorations that oscillated in the breeze.

It is amazing that the statues of so many members of one family were discovered. After studying their statues for a while, you feel as if they are about to come to life. It becomes easy to visualize the real-life Balbuses engaged in activities throughout the Town of Hercules: Balbus the Younger competing in the sports arena; the proconsul strutting about the Forum; the mother gossiping at the Baths; the girls shopping; the whole family displaying themselves at the Theater; all of them dining in the fountain-splashed courtyard of their luxurious house above the marina.

What a sight, to have been present when the marble Balbuses emerged from centuries of darkness in the Basilica into the glaring light of day! Larger-than-life versions of the family moved through the streets of the town that the flesh-and-blood Balbuses had known so well. Twenty centuries ago, did the Balbus men and women escape Herculaneum in time to live out their lives elsewhere? A funeral altar in town is evidence that Balbus the Elder had died shortly before Vesuvius erupted. As to the fate of other family members, not a clue remains.

SPORTS: THE PALAESTRA

In Herculaneum's sports complex, athletes could swim, run foot races, lift weights, play ball games, wrestle, box, and engage in many other forms of exercise and competition.

Romans believed that healthy bodies made healthy minds. One of their favorite sayings was: "A sound mind in a sound body" (*Mens sana in corpore sano*). Earlier, the Greeks had the same idea. In southern Italy, the Greek tradition of the Olympic Games blended with the Roman practice of holding sporting events at festivals to stress healthy bodies.

The importance of sports is made clear by the huge size of the Palaestra, a sports arena and public gymnasium, in a town as small as Herculaneum. To the Spanish tunnelers, the Palaestra was bewildering. They thought they had stumbled on a great temple or a vast private villa. Today's visitor can hardly believe what he sees. The arena is larger than an entire modern city block.

Within, a columned enclosed walkway surrounded the open sports area on three sides. On the north, or shady, side, a portico and a loggia provided a comfortable place for officials and special guests to watch the competitions. Next to the loggia was

In the grand hall of the Palaestra, or sports arena, a statue of Hercules almost certainly stood in the huge niche. This is where winning athletes were awarded the olive-wreath crowns of victory. The wreaths were probably placed on the massive marble table while the nude athletes marched into the hall to the strains of music. The Palaestra's second story and ceiling did not survive excavation; the section shown here is 40 feet high.

These statues may be two boy wrestlers about to close in on one another in friendly combat. (Scholars aren't sure; the statues may depict runners about to start a race.) Before a match, naked wrestlers would smear their skin with a mixture of oil and wax. Then they sprinkled on a light coating of dust so they wouldn't slip from each other's grasp.

a large and elegant meeting hall that could seat hundreds. As yet, only two sides of this hall have been completely excavated. It was in one of these rooms that Spanish excavators scratched their names and the date, *1750.*

The main entrance to the Palaestra is like the majestic entrance to a great temple. But the tunnelers burrowed through the vaulted entrance, and when the volcanic mass was removed the ceiling collapsed. Fortunately, other parts of the structure escaped this kind of destruction.

Although now roofless, the main hall is still about four stories in height. This was the hall where victorious athletes received their awards. A huge niche at the back almost certainly contained an enormous statue of the patron of the games, Hercules. As in other Roman palaestras, a statue of Hygeia, the goddess of health, stood on one side. (Our word *hygiene* is derived from the name of this goddess.)

In front of the niche where the statue of Hercules once stood, a large, heavy marble table, with legs carved in the shape of eagles' claws, now remains. It was on this table that the victors' sole rewards—their wreaths—were placed. Each wreath was made from branches cut from a wild olive tree, the same tree that gave Hercules his clubs. It was an ancient Greek custom that a healthy boy whose parents were both living would cut the wreaths with a golden knife.

Into the main hall marched all the athletes to stand before the statue of Hercules. They were naked and glistened from the olive oil on their bronzed skin. Their march was accompanied by the music of trumpets and the cheers of spectators. All sought the blessing of Hercules at the beginning of the games. In this hall sacrifices probably were offered, usually young goats or lambs.

By the first century of our era, many educated Romans no longer placed the slightest faith in such rituals. Nevertheless, here stood the priests of Hercules, arms raised and palms held upward. Entrails were inspected to learn if the sacrifice was pleasing to the gods. Smoke from incense and the burning sacrifice rose before the image of the hero-god. Then the boys and young men marched out again, around the whole arena. To the music of flutes the games began.

The sports events were paid for by a wealthy citizen, usually a patrician. The feasts that followed were paid for by rich freedmen. We know that the Proconsul Balbus was one of those who sponsored the Herculaneum games. On the day of Vesuvius's eruption, a stone-toss competition must have been under way. The excavators found round stones, weighing about 5 pounds each, laid out for use.

The playing field itself was spacious. There was plenty of room for a row of towering umbrella pines. (Evidence of their roots has been found.) The field was large enough for all the exhibition sports: foot races, wrestling, boxing, discus

The Palaestra's playing field was dominated by an impressive cross-shaped pool adorned with a five-headed statue of a serpent. Runners may have raced around the field's perimeter, in the shaded path lined with columns. The function of the deep and narrow second pool remains a mystery.

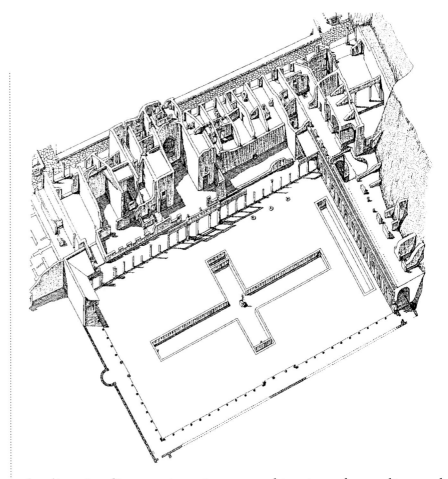

hurling, javelin toss, jumping, a combination of wrestling and boxing, and a series of five contests for all-around athletes—the pentathlon. (In boxing, victory did not depend on a knockout but on a blow to the head. The loser raised a finger to signal defeat.) All athletes had to swear that they had been in training for ten months.

Herculaneum's Palaestra seems to have been modeled on the Palaestra at the Greek city of Olympia, which was the site of the ancient Olympic games. As water was plentiful in Herculaneum, swimming contests must have been added. (A painting in an early Greek tomb near Herculaneum shows a tanned young man making a high dive from a platform.)

In the center of the Palaestra's playing field, a large, cross-shaped swimming pool was found. It is about 160 feet long, with a cross arm of about 100 feet. At each end was a fountain. In the center, a giant bronze serpent coiled on the limbs of a bronze tree. The serpent, too, was a fountain—from five crowned heads water sprayed into the pool. This pool typifies the Roman desire to make public places beautiful.

Another pool was discovered in the Palaestra. Before it was fully excavated, it was thought to be a pool for children's competitions. But we now know that use by children was unlikely because of the pool's depth—more than the height of a man. It was also very narrow, and would have been dangerous for high divers. A series of underwater niches in the pool run all the way down to the bottom. So far, nobody has been able to explain what the second pool, with its unusual features, might have been used for.

A mountain of hardened volcanic matter still fills and covers the cross-shaped pool. So far, it is merely hollowed out like a cavern over the central portion. To walk the full length of the pool you must go through tunnels. It is in the tunnels that you best realize the volume of the volcanic mass and its force. Carbonized beams, chunks of marble, bits of mosaics, fallen columns—all are scattered as if stirred by a giant child into an enormous mud pie, then baked dry and hard. Here the pyroclastic flow was at its swiftest and most forceful.

Only the word "terrifying" can describe the scene as you pass through. And you regret that this beautiful pool is not once more open to the sun and air. But, someday, the whole sports area may again be on view. And perhaps games will be held there, the way ancient plays are now sometimes performed in the Theater of Pompeii. Perhaps young athletes from all over the world will compete at Herculaneum. We may safely assume that the good citizens of Herculaneum would approve.

AT THE BATHS

A visit to one of the town's two public baths was a time for socializing, playing games, exercising, and leisurely soaking or swimming in a series of warm, hot, and cold communal pools.

Bathing, for the Romans, was not a chore but a pleasant social event, almost like going to a party. The baths were places for cleanliness, fitness, and fun. Young and old, rich and poor—almost everybody went at least once a day.

Few houses needed private baths. None could compare with the attractions of the public baths. Some were town-owned and some were private enterprises. The public baths were used collectively. Many were more elaborate and better equipped than modern country clubs. The citizens of Herculaneum, like the citizens of Rome, loved the baths and valued cleanliness. We can only marvel at what they built: lovely buildings with a variety of vaulted, beautifully decorated rooms and pleasant outdoor spaces. All of it was engineered to provide the convenience of running water and the comfort of central heat.

The human body was an object of admiration and respect to the Romans, as to the Greeks. Both cultures produced

While they bided their time on marble benches in the waiting room of the Suburban Baths, Herculaneum's residents could admire well-crafted stucco wall decorations. This photograph shows a Greek warrior and two plump cupids. (Stucco decorations are extremely fragile, and only a few examples have survived from ancient times.) Rock-hard volcanic material still clings to the original wooden door.

great sculpture and paintings idealizing the human form. Nudity was accepted as a natural state. In early Roman times, people bathed without clothing. Later, women wore a light covering garment while bathing in mixed company, and men wore brief leather loincloths. Later still, it was forbidden for men and women to bathe together. In small towns, as at Herculaneum, men and women had separate sections of the baths or used the same sections at different hours. Poor and rich mingled. The well-to-do were accompanied by their slaves.

Almost all baths were equipped with a gymnasium and with courts for ball games. Before bathing, Roman citizens would undress in a special room. Then they might go to the gym or ball courts to exercise vigorously and work up a good sweat. A favorite game was bladder-ball (*pila*), played with inflated animal bladders that were often painted green. Other games used sand-filled or feather-filled balls. In one, an enormous ball filled with dirt or flour was pummeled like a huge punching bag. Romans also liked to work out with weights, jog, or run races. Women favored a game called hoops, in which they used a little curved stick to roll a large metal hoop along the ground. By the end of the first century A.D., exercise attracted more and more girls and women. They not only played hoops but also went in for ball games and fencing.

When the exercises were completed, the baths began. Sometimes the sequence of activities might vary, but usually Romans followed their workout on the yard with a cleansing rubdown. Slaves would apply a mixture of olive oil and finely ground pumice to a patron's body, then scrape off the dirt, oil, and sweat with a strigil. This was a curved implement made of bone or bronze that somewhat resembled a small boomerang.

Next came the baths themselves. The tepidarium was a

warm room and the caldarium a hot, steam-filled room with a bath "tub" and a separate fountain for washing. From the warm or hot room, bathers hurried into the cold room (frigidarium) for a dip in its cold-water plunge. The plunge was usually the size of a small pool, deep enough for people to immerse their bodies.

After the cold dip, some patrons enjoyed having slaves give them another quick rubdown. Romans were not content with a fresh-scrubbed odor, so perfume was used by both women and men. Then they dressed and relaxed in the garden, conversing with friends and playing dice or board games.

Snacks, eaten with a little wine, were provided for patrons who were hungry. Some baths had "relaxing rooms" for those who wished to hear poetry recited. Some also had private dining rooms for special parties. Many had libraries and reading rooms filled with papyrus scrolls, the Roman form of books.

Every effort was made to decorate the baths as beautifully as possible, with wall paintings, mosaics, statues, and architectural details. Many baths had arcades or garden paths for strolling among flowers, fountains and music to soothe nerves, and galleries filled with statues and paintings to charm the eye. A visit to the baths was cleansing, refreshing, and pleasing to body and spirit.

A set of metal bath utensils consists of four curved strigils hanging from a ring. After oil was rubbed on the bather's body, the curved part of the strigil was used to scrape sweat and grime from the skin. Later, more oil and perfume were applied.

Herculaneum was a small town, yet it had two sets of baths. One, now known as the Forum Baths, was near the center of town. The other, now known as the Suburban Baths, was at the marina, outside the old town walls.

The Forum Baths occupied the southern end of a whole

Herculaneum's Forum Baths. By Roman standards it was a modest establishment, with a small central Palaestra, or sports area. Men and women had separate rooms.

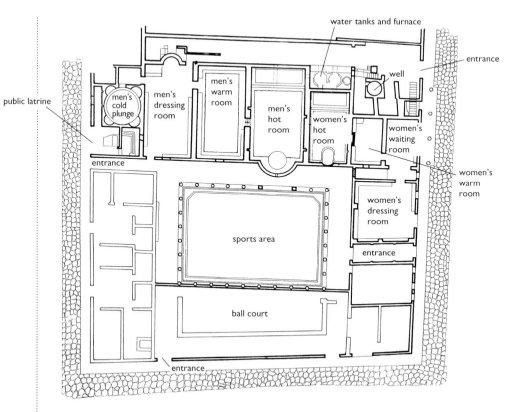

block, fronting on three different streets. It had several entrances. A patron could go directly to the open-air gymnasium if he wished. The main hall has preserved the usual graffiti and scribbles drawn by people bored with waiting—names in Latin and Greek mingled with doodles. The garden was surrounded by a columned walkway. To one side was an open exercise and playing area. This space was not big enough for ball games, so a covered court was built on an upper story.

On the walls of the waiting room to the woman's section, Herculaneum's citizens scratched messages to one another. One was a scrawled salute to the poet Ovid, who wrote *The Art of Love*. Others were a sketch of a naked girl, several phallic good-luck charms, and the Latin alphabet as far as *Q*. Perhaps that was the letter on which Vesuvius exploded.

The Forum Baths were about 100 years old at the time of the eruption. Their plan follows the standard Roman pattern. Off one entrance is a doorkeeper's cubicle and the public latrine. The latrine was flushed with water flowing from the cold plunge—an example of Roman ingenuity in conserving natural resources. In the men's dressing room a marble bench runs around three sides, and a marble shelf has individual spaces for clothing. The ceiling is vaulted and the pavement is made of irregular pieces of black, gray, and white marble—the inexpensive scrap. The floor is slightly curved, like a bowl, to make it easier to wash and drain. A white marble basin stands at one end of the room; in a corner, another basin is set lower down. The first was used for washing hands, the second for washing feet before entering the other chambers of the Baths. The entire room was lighted (and heated) by a large round window high in the south wall.

In this room five skeletons were found—four men and a woman. They did not flee, perhaps thinking they would be safe high on a shelf under the massive thickness of the vaulted ceiling. They certainly did not expect a churning river of volcanic debris to engulf them there, but that is what happened.

The warm room opens off the dressing room. The floor, supported by pillars, had hollow spaces beneath it to allow for the passage of hot air. It collapsed under the weight of the pyroclastic flow that filled the room. But the mosaic design adorning the now-sunken floor is almost undamaged—a huge Triton, with legs of curling sea serpents, surrounded by leaping dolphins.

Next to the warm room is the hot room. Here the vaulted ceiling collapsed, revealing terra-cotta hot-air pipes in the walls. At one end, a large marble basin that looks like a birdbath contained cold water to wash sweat from the eyes. At the other end

In the women's dressing room of the Forum Baths (right), sea creatures swirl around Triton, son of Neptune, in a dramatic floor mosaic. A marble shelf with dividers functioned as "lockers" for Herculaneum's ladies.

A view of the women's caldarium of the Forum Baths (above) shows the hot-water pool that stretches along the entire back wall. The vaulted, or arched, ceiling has a simple design of stucco grooving.

was the hot-water plunge. In the hot rooms of Roman baths, the heating system was so efficient that patrons wore wooden sandals to protect the soles of their feet from the hot floor.

The circular cold room had a cold-water plunge. It also had seats in niches for those who wanted to rest. Bronze candelabra indicate that the plunge was used at night. The walls are painted dark red, the niches golden yellow. On the blue-gray vaulted ceiling a painting of marine creatures shows fish, lobsters, and a moray eel being captured by an octopus. When no one was swimming, images of sea life reflected in the water of the green pool below.

The women's section of the Forum Baths is similar to the men's—another Triton decorates the changing room—but the women's side lacks a cold room and a cold plunge. There are more hot-water pipes in the walls on this side than in the men's section, and the women had a separate boiler for their unit. Apparently, Herculaneum's ladies did not enjoy a frigidarium and liked their water hotter than the men did.

The Forum Baths are typical of a standard establishment, but the Suburban Baths are very much out of the ordinary. Their location is unusual. They were built just outside the town walls with a view of the marina—like an elegant yacht club. The arrangement of rooms and the decorations are unique, too. In fact, no similar public baths are known to have survived anywhere, so they are one of the great finds of archaeology. Their state of preservation, in spite of exceptional difficulties in digging, is remarkable.

The entrance courtyard to the Suburban Baths is a terrace. In it stood an honorary memorial to Proconsul Balbus as well as a statue of him. The statue was swept away during the eruption; it was only recently uncovered on the beach. The memorial inscription states that Balbus, at his own expense, restored the Basilica, gates, and walls of the town after the great earthquake. A list of his titles is given. Balbus sponsored youth games and helped erect a colossal statue of the Emperor Vespasian. Judging from the location of the proconsul's statue, it seems likely that he also gave the Suburban Baths to the town. His own house appears to have been next door, above the town wall, with connecting ramps. The proconsul's many acts of patronage must have been well appreciated by citizens of

The men's hot room (caldarium) of the Forum Baths was heated using a system of clay hot-air pipes installed beneath the floor and inside the walls. A section of pipe is clearly visible in the left foreground of this photograph. After a dip, bathers would refresh themselves with cool water from a basin that stood in the semicircular niche at the far end of the room.

Herculaneum. As we saw in Chapter 10, the entire Balbus family was honored at the Basilica, where statues of each member were publicly displayed.

Although the volcanic avalanche swept away the walls of nearby houses, the snugly placed Suburban Baths lost hardly a stone. The pyroclastic flow solidified and the water table changed. The hard ground and problems with water seepage made excavations slow and difficult. The dig could not be completed until a modern automatic pumping system was installed. Otherwise, present visitors would be sloshing about in four or five feet of water. This very pumping system led to the dramatic discoveries of many Roman skeletons at the marina, already discussed in Chapter 6.

At the entrance to the Suburban Baths, four massive red columns stand at the corners of a square white marble fountain, where water once flowed from a statue of the sun god Apollo, a fine Greek sculpture. (The Roman valve still works.) Light comes from a skylight placed above four rows of arches, showing that the architect was both daring and skillful. All the doors and windows have wide wooden frames similar to large frames for paintings in museums.

A dressing room flanks each side of the entrance stairway. Here patrons removed and stored their clothing and wrapped themselves in a linen cloth or towel. Then they went on to a waiting room. This room was heated in winter by hot-air pipes in the walls that worked somewhat like modern radiant heating systems. The waiting room was one of the most exciting finds ever made by archeologists. It looked exactly as it did 2,000 years ago, except that the Spanish tunnelers had destroyed decorations on the vaulted ceiling. Luckily, they had not burrowed deeper into the room itself.

Herculaneum's well-to-do citizens entered the Suburban Baths through this light-filled vestibule, where a marble bust of Apollo greeted them.

Light enters through a glass-enclosed window built into a niche in the ceiling. The pavement is made of black marble squares separated by white marble bands. Three walls have white marble benches set against many-colored marble backgrounds. The naked warriors formed in stucco are what make this room so remarkable. The warriors, about 2½ feet high in framed panels, are the work of a first-class artist. They were hardly damaged by the eruption. Even the handsomely paneled wooden doors remain on their original hinges in their original places.

In the warm room, the walls are covered with paintings

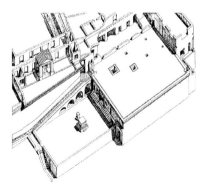

Men and women did not have separate sections at the Suburban Baths, so they must have used the facility at different times. This drawing shows the large courtyard where a statue of Proconsul Balbus once stood.

of fantastic architecture that looks like something from a dream. Inset terra-cotta tubes or pipes heat the walls and room. The swimming pool, too, is heated. To one side is a small round sweat room with seats in niches, like a modern sauna. It was as finely decorated as a jewel cabinet.

The hot room has a marble pool for hot water and a round marble basin for cold water. Here the power of Vesuvius is dramatically illustrated. The volcano delivered an avalanche of hot ash and gases that rushed in through the window and overturned the massive marble basin. Then the flow shoved the basin across the room and left it stranded, balanced on edge, with a trail of broken glass behind.

The plunge, or pool, in the cold room is faced with red marble and has white marble steps and a white marble bottom. It's quite a fancy swimming pool, anywhere, anytime. Few people swim in anything like it today.

The lounge was used for relaxing and chatting, perhaps while enjoying a snack and a glass of wine. It had two large picture windows overlooking the sea and a third overlooking the marina. The furniture probably consisted of wicker chairs set beside small round tables. The handsome wall decorations are now badly damaged.

The Suburban Baths offer additional surprises. The furnace room is complete with its pipes and boiler; wood is still piled neatly on the floor. Water was piped in from the town aqueduct. In one room, a heap of unbroken hollow bricks remain; they were being used for repairs. In the back corridor, wooden scaffolding is still stacked against the wall, uncharred. Also unscorched are wooden shutters that look exactly like those on early-American and modern houses. Thirty-five roof tiles are stamped with an abbreviated version of the name of the craftsman who manufactured them: *M AC AMP*, for Marcus Accius Ampliatus.

At the end of the corridor was a private dining or party room. Funsters drew caricatures of two friends on the wall. A lady is shown with her nose comically prolonged, wearing a crown of vine leaves. A gentleman is drawn with an absurdly receding chin, wearing an affected, high-combed, curled hairdo.

These white walls seem to have been as tempting as a modern blackboard. A slave left this record of his visit: "I, Hermeros, slave of my mistress Primagenia, came from Puteoli to Timnianus Street and am looking for the bank messenger, the slave of Phoebus."

Another graffito relates: "Two companions were here. After the bad guidance of Epaphroditus in everything, they tardily threw him out. Then with the girls they joyfully consumed 105½ sesterces." Sesterces were one unit of Roman money, and that amount indicates that the party was a fairly expensive one. A list of what was eaten—twelve pizzas (Roman *offellae*)—is also recorded on the wall. Sexually explicit graffiti, probably scrawled by Romans who had been drinking a little too much wine, provide further evidence that the Suburban Baths were a lively place from any point of view.

Graffiti written in Latin were found on a wall in a back room of the Suburban Baths. Perhaps the lady caricatured was the famous beauty from Pompeii, Primagenia, whose name was scratched elsewhere on the the wall. Party-goers kept a tally list of what they ate: the Roman numeral XII next to the third entry means that twelve *offellae*, or Roman pizzas, were consumed.

13

SHOW TIME: THE THEATER

Roman and Greek plays were produced for large, enthusiastic crowds at Herculaneum's elegant Theater. A rehearsal was probably just finishing when Vesuvius made its awesome presence known on August 24, A.D. 79.

Ancient Romans would feel perfectly at home on New York's Broadway, and if we could travel back through time to the Town of Hercules of 2,000 years ago both the Theater itself and the performances would have many familiar qualities. Roman drama and the Roman theater are the direct ancestors of our own. At the same time, some aspects of Roman entertainment would have struck us with their novelty.

The Herculaneum Theater is the only ancient theater thus far discovered intact. During the eruption, volcanic matter rose higher and higher outside the Theater until it reached the top. Then it flowed over the upper edge, filling the semicircular structure like a huge bowl. Only the statuary around the edges was swept away. All else was preserved.

You may recall that the accidental discovery of fine marble in 1709 by surprised well-diggers marked the beginning of the plunder and, later on, the exploration of Herculaneum and Pompeii. The site of that original discovery was the

The Player King, a small painting from Herculaneum, portrays a group of actors backstage, with their masks off. The brooding actor on the left remains in costume after playing a royal role. A woman kneels beneath a theatrical mask. In the background, another actor changes costume. With its skillfully applied and delicate colors, this is one of the most famous paintings surviving from ancient times.

The grandeur of a Roman theater's elaborate stage set is depicted in this mural from Herculaneum's Basilica. The painting shows a stage's permanent backdrop, which has been built and decorated to resemble a palace's ornate entrance.

Herculaneum Theater, although it was not identified as such until almost thirty years afterward. Unfortunately for us, the Theater was looted for many years by princes and kings, who used it merely as a source of precious marbles, statuary, and jewels. For almost forty years, the tunneling in and out of the Theater went on, despite the fact that the structure was buried under 60 to 90 feet of hardened mud.

Modern archaeologists say that in less time, and probably at no greater cost, the whole theater could have been uncovered. If it had been revealed and not plundered, it would be today one of the archaeological wonders of the world. We would have seen an important Greek-Roman theater at the moment of rehearsal for an afternoon performance. Theatrical shows were usually part of festivals, and on the day Vesuvius erupted people were celebrating the birthday of the deified Emperor Augustus.

Old Greek dramas as well as Roman plays were favored by the Greek-speaking people of southern Italy. Because Herculaneum was close to Naples, it probably drew the best troupes of actors from Athens, Alexandria (the famed Greek city in Egypt), and Rome. Like tragedy, comedy and farce were in great demand. Except for gladiatorial combats and chariot races, pantomimes were the most popular of all spectacles.

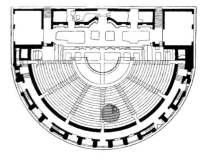

A model and floor plan of Herculaneum's impressive open-air Theater. In its day, the D-shaped building was adorned with marble and bronze statues. Now the looted ruins are buried under 60 to 90 feet of volcanic rock. A circle on the plan shows where the well shaft dug in 1709 met the upper level of marble seats.

A wooden flute and its mouthpiece, found in Herculaneum, make up just one of many musical instruments used in Roman theater. Musical comedies called pantomimes required an orchestra, with trumpets, pipes, zithers, lyres, drums, and cymbals.

Little or no spoken dialogue was used in the pantomimes. Actors used gestures and body language to play their roles. Singing and dancing were the important parts.

During the course of Roman history, theater underwent changes. In the old Roman theater, all roles had been played by males. But later, actresses came into their own, especially in the pantomimes. In the beginning, masks—tragic and comic—had been worn by all actors. Eventually, they were dropped, and actors faced the audience just as performers do today. (Masks were in use in Herculaneum.) Successful actors and mimes were idolized the way movie stars are now. They commanded big money and had fashionable friends—sometimes even emperors and empresses. All the same, laws discriminated against actors, and they were set apart from the rest of the population.

By the year of Vesuvius's eruption, the pantomime had become very similar to modern American musical comedy. Leading actors and actresses were singing and dancing stars. Costumes often were scanty, especially for chorus girls. For some parts, nothing at all was worn. A male role, such as Apollo, was played without costume, as was Venus and other goddesses. Essential in all comedy was the double-meaning gag and gesture, which drew laughter from the noisy and enthusiastic audiences.

Imagine the Herculaneum Theater on the day of a performance: Yellow and blue awnings were slung from masts across the whole structure to protect the audience from the sun, and many-colored cushions made the stone seats more comfortable. Attendants sprayed saffron-scented water from skin bottles to freshen the heavy air, while vendors hawked trays of sweets and nuts. People quarreled over seats. Children curiously examined the machinery for lowering the curtain into the pit and tried to locate trap doors on the stage. Creaky cranes helped the gods "fly" through space, and huge bronze drums created the sound of thunder. Scenery revolved. Musicians played a wide variety of musical instruments. Backstage, actors adjusted their costumes, masks, wigs, powder, and other makeup. An air of excitement infected both the performers and the crowd of spectators who flocked to the Theater. Once a performance was underway, an enthusiastic crowd would roar its approval.

The Herculaneum Theater is considered an architectural jewel. It seated 2,500 people—a large number considering the town probably had only twice that many residents. After the fall of Rome, theaters such as this were not to be seen again until the 1500s. The Herculaneum Theater had been built in the time of the Emperor Augustus. It was not cut into a hillside, as theaters in Greece and Pompeii were, but stood independently, like the theaters of Naples and Rome. It was, however, a semicircle supported by arches and pillars. All the decorations were very rich.

The stage displayed the true pomp of the building. It had a permanent backdrop embellished with rare marbles and statuary. Walls and columns of the stone and plaster scenery were faced with marbles of black, yellow, purple, and red. Some were faced with alabaster. As in other Roman theaters, a second curtain was probably sometimes raised up in front so that painted scenery could be used. The Romans always liked realism in theatrical settings.

Above the orchestra, stone seats filled the auditorium in semicircular tiers. Flights of steps led to the various seat groupings. The first four rows were reserved for local magistrates, officials from Rome, and distinguished citizens. The next sixteen rows were reserved for aristocrats. A barrier about a yard high separated the first twenty rows from the rest of the theater. Ordinary citizens, including women and children, sat behind the barrier.

The most important officials sat in boxes over entrances to the orchestra, at either end of the stage. One no doubt was reserved for Proconsul Balbus and his family, for his rank was far above that of any local magistrate. In Roman theaters, all seats were free, and only slaves were barred.

Theater exits (at Herculaneum there were seven) were called *vomitoria*. Guards at Herculaneum and Pompeii enjoy teasing modern visitors who wonder where the name came from. They tell the tourists that the Romans gorged themselves at meals, then vomited to eat more. (This is not really true.) Then the guards identify various open holes in private houses as vomitoria. This is a good example of the way misinformation is circulated. Of course, Romans did not vomit in these passages. Theater exits were called vomitoria because their function was to "disgorge" spectators when the show was over.

Today, the original well shaft and tunnels through the Theater remain much as they were when the explorations were abandoned. A visitor receives a vivid impression of the conditions of Neapolitan diggers working deep underground. Mists and vapors slither through the corridors, appearing and disappearing. Water and slime drip from the ceilings and walls. The air is dank, bone-chilling. Squeaking bats dart from the darkness. Even with electric lights, the tunnels disappear abruptly into the mysterious tomblike darkness of twenty centuries. The imprint of a statue's face in the hardened mud looks like a demonic leer. Reverberating echoes sound like the screams of a crowd in panic. Someday, we hope, all this will change. When complete excavation again opens the Theater, a living audience will be inspired to imagine the excitement of the greatest plays of antiquity.

14

MAIN STREET

With its shaded walkways, fountains, public buildings, stores, and workshops, this wide pedestrian promenade attracted a lively crowd of people.

Romans, as great organizers, considered a town without a Forum not a town at all. The Forum was the center of civic life, of banking, of trade. The Forum was a place for people to meet and talk about business and politics—and also to gossip.

In spite of the maze of tunnels and shafts, early information gained about Herculaneum's Forum was scanty. Yet a town with public buildings as impressive as the Palaestra, Basilica, and two public baths was sure to have an equally impressive Forum.

When Main Street was discovered, it seemed likely that the Forum would not be far away. A map from the 1700s (drawn on the basis of the tunnels) showed a main street and an open area that might have been the Forum. But the map was not exact. Unfortunately, both Main Street and the Forum appeared to be under a heavily populated residential area of Resina. Before excavations could begin, houses had to be torn down. It has been a slow and costly process, and

A sign from Herculaneum's Main Street beckons customers to a wine shop with the words *Ad Cucumas*. That's Latin for "Come to the Sign of the Wine Bowls!" Beneath the jugs are names and vintages of various wines for sale.

Townspeople once flocked to the shops and houses that line Main Street's wide expanse. Beyond the arch at the far end of the street lie the Forum and perhaps a great temple, but they remain locked in a wall of volcanic rock. Buildings in the modern city of Ercolano, seen here above the arch, would be endangered by future digging.

only part of Main Street has been uncovered. The Forum is yet to come.

Compared with other streets of Herculaneum, Main Street is very wide—about 40 feet, including sidewalks of 10 or 12 feet on each side. The street was a pedestrian's paradise: Carts, wagons, and chariots were prevented from entering the area by stone steps or pillars built at either end.

Smooth Vesuvian stones pave the street itself. The curbstones are low and the gutters are made of brick. On the southern side, the sidewalk was protected from the sun by overhanging roofs, some of which were supported by carved wooden beams that are still visible. On the north, a

covered walkway with columns protected shoppers from rainy weather. Here, excavators found a partially open crate of fine glassware. But volcanic matter still fills the house or shop that it came from.

Main Street begins with a small public square in front of the assembly hall of the sports arena. It is marked by a public fountain. A jet of water spurts from a crudely carved head of Hercules into a rectangular trough. Farther down the street is another fountain, this one with an image of Venus. People whose homes or apartments were not hooked up to the system of aqueducts could draw water from the town's public fountains. Nearby is a painted shrine with serpents. Smaller streets

A reconstruction of Main Street shows the long awning that shaded half the street. Townspeople could draw water from the rectangular stone fountain in the foreground. The stone pillar in the middle of the street prevented carts and chariots from entering.

Roman stone reliefs show what work-shops and stores along Main Street might have looked like. Using his heavy hammer, the blacksmith, seated, pounds hot metal against the anvil. He is flanked by his young helper on the left and by his tools and metal-work on the right.

lead down toward the waterfront. Town "bulletin boards" in the form of stone pillars were placed at these intersections. Notices were written right on the stone. One pillar carries a town ordinance against litterbugs—the penalty for littering was a fine or a whipping, or both.

A continuous line of shops and workshops opened on both sides of the street. Mixed in was an occasional patrician house. One typical workshop was the metalsmith's, where a bronze statuette of Bacchus was found still waiting for repair. At another shop, an artist in the process of painting a panel of cupids left his handiwork unfinished.

Advertising here is restrained. For example, in a wine shop a painting shows Bacchus with a half-dozen samples of various types of wines. The clear meaning is that these wines are fit for a god. The slogan is short and modern: "Come to the Sign of the Wine Bowls!" (Romans drank wine from bowls, not cups or glasses.)

The map from the 1700s indicates that a great temple stood at the end of Main Street, but no temple has yet been found. Perhaps the street is a very long one, and the temple remains far away. At the end of the short section already exca-vated, a massive arch with vaults opening on all four sides dominates the street. Originally, it was faced with marble, embellished with stucco decorations, and had four equestrian bronzes. It was an imposing arch, similar to those in ancient Rome and to modern, single- or double-vaulted arches in Paris and New York. In the 1700s, it was stripped of its beautiful statues and plaster decorations, and only traces remain.

Across the street is one of the structures most recently excavated: the Shrine of the Augustales. It was the headquarters of the Augustales, officials responsible for worship of the deified emperors. This religion served a definite political purpose. It attempted to establish a single unifying religion among all the different peoples of the Roman Empire. (Emperor worship was not unlike the unifying role of the Royal Family in the former British Empire.)

The Augustales were established in A.D. 14 by a decree of the Senate deifying the dead Emperor Augustus—that is, declaring that he was a god. Subsequent emperors were so powerful, so glorified, and so elevated that it was easy for distant peoples to accept them as gods. The emperors had assumed the title *Pontifex Maximus,* or High Priest, of the Roman religion. (The Roman Catholic Pope carries the same title today.) So deification was but one more step. The Emperor Vespasian died only a month before the eruption. As death approached, he moaned, "Alas! I must be turning into a god!" It was his last joke. He had been called "sacred" while he was still alive.

In Herculaneum, the Augustales headquarters has an inscription stating that the first banquet was given by "Proculus and Julian." That banquet was probably a rowdy party—Roman men did not like to be somber at meals. The tunnelers stripped the hall of everything except the inscription.

The Augustales have left us a mystery. One portion of the hall was closed off by a temporary partition of trellis construction. This formed a small room with only one door and

At the butcher's, a woman holding her shopping list sits patiently while the butcher uses a cleaver to prepare a slab of meat.

Young boys and small children learn their father's trade in a scene depicting a coppersmith's workshop.

This beautiful room, the Shrine of the
Augustales, was dedicated to the
deified emperors (including Augustus)
in accordance with the official religion
of Rome. To the right is a locked room
where the skeleton of a man was found
lying face down on an expensive bed.

one tiny barred window that looked inward into the hall. In
this room there are only two pieces of furniture: a bed and a
table. Both are made of wood and are of fine quality.

On the bed is the skeleton of a man. He seems to have
thrown himself face down—hopelessly waiting for the final
volcanic surge. Who was this man? Why did he fail to escape?

He was trapped because the door was locked. Was he a political prisoner? Was he an important man—too important to occupy an ordinary jail? Was he kept under lock and key by members of his own class? Sometimes, the behind-the-scenes political dealings of the Roman ruling class led to extreme situations. Banishment, house arrest, and forced changes of residence had occurred. The man in the locked room might have been an unpopular member of the Augustales in Rome who had been sent to the Augustales in Herculaneum "for his own protection." Perhaps someday a chance reference will provide the key to that strange little room—and its prisoner who has lain in a position of despair for almost 2,000 years.

15

A COUNTRY TREASURE HOUSE

An opulent suburban villa discovered outside Herculaneum more than 200 years ago is still completely buried, but halfway around the world a full-scale adaptation is open to the public: the J. Paul Getty Museum in Malibu, California.

Very, very rich Romans lived in the luxurious country house now called the Villa of the Papyri. Ancient Romans referred to their large suburban retreats, which consisted of a house with beautifully decorated gardens, as villas. This one gets its name from the books in its library, written on scrolls made of the Egyptian material called papyrus. So the name really means "Villa of the Book Rolls."

The Villa of the Papyri was completely buried by the A.D. 79 eruption of Vesuvius, and it remains covered by hardened pyroclastic flow to this day. In 1752, it was discovered a short distance away from Herculaneum and was explored through tunnels. The excavation tunnels were sealed in 1765. Although people knew approximately where the Villa was buried, its exact location was eventually forgotten. It wasn't until the 1980s that modern archaeologists rediscovered the Villa's whereabouts; on October 16, 1986, people entered it for the first time in 221 years. The tunnels were reopened for

At the J. Paul Getty Museum, visitors can walk back through time to the Villa of the Papyri. This is a photograph of the museum's main peristyle garden, complete with a 217-foot-long reflecting pool, authentic Roman plantings, and reproductions of statues from the Villa. In the foreground, a life-size bronze statue shows an old faun leaning back and snapping his fingers in a gesture of drunken abandon.

Nestled into a hillside overlooking the sea, the J. Paul Getty Museum (above) re-creates the general setting and many details of the luxurious Villa of the Papyri. The museum's layout is based on a plan (right) of the still-buried Villa originally drawn by Karl Weber in the 1750s.

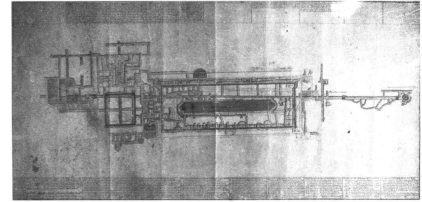

exploration, but removing the 65 to 85 feet of volcanic matter still entombing the Villa would be a major project.

Luckily, the Swiss architect Karl Weber had drawn a detailed plan during the original tunneling in the 1750s. Weber's plan provided a wealth of specific information about the Villa and its gardens, and it eventually became the basic inspiration for the J. Paul Getty Museum in Malibu, California. Many of the treasures from the Villa may be seen in the National Archaeological Museum in Naples, and fine reproductions of about half are on display in the Getty Museum.

The Villa was a low structure of red-tiled roofs and columned walkways surrounding gardens, fountains, and pools. The whole complex stretched at least 800 feet along an embankment above the Bay of Naples. Below it was a beach with private docks. Stairs and terraces led upward from the bay to the Villa level. The entrance had impressive columns.

In the Villa, the old-fashioned atrium of a "typical" Roman house was transformed into a large entrance hall. In the middle of its black-and-white mosaic pavement was the familiar rainwater catch-basin, but here the marble pool was surrounded by eleven statues. Five of the statues were fountains taking the form of seated silens, or old satyrs, pouring water from wineskins or panthers' mouths. Two were young fauns pouring water from the mouths of wineskins. Jets of water all around the pool transformed it into a fanciful fountain. (Silens, satyrs, and fauns are mythological woodland creatures that display earthy desires and behaviors. They are usually portrayed as little men with tails, horns, shaggy hair, and other goatlike or horselike features.)

> **KEY DATES**

A.D. 79   Mount Vesuvius erupts; the Villa of the Papyri is engulfed in pyroclastic flows.

1750s   Well-diggers discover the Villa beneath 65 feet of volcanic rock in 1750. Under the direction of Karl Weber, workers build tunnels, begin to mine the Villa for treasures. In 1754, a library of books written on about 1,800 papyrus scrolls is discovered.

1760s   Work on the Villa proceeds in fits and starts. In 1765, all tunnels are sealed to contain poisonous gases, and all exploration ceases.

1800s   The Villa's precise location is forgotten, although its general vicinity is still known.

1974   The J. Paul Getty Museum (above) opens in Malibu, California.

1980s   The Villa's exact location is rediscovered. In 1986, archaeologists reenter the Villa of the Papyri.

A fresco from Pompeii shows what a Roman villa looked like.

The large basin of another fountain was nestled in a wall niche where thirteen bronze panthers spurted water from their mouths. Other niches housed busts of Greek rulers and philosophers and statuettes of mythical creatures, including a dancing young faun and a bearded, pipe-playing satyr.

The entrance hall opened directly into a square courtyard with ten columns on each side—the inner peristyle garden. In the middle, streams of water splashed from conch shells into a long, narrow pool. Here, excavators found the bronze head of *The Spear Bearer*, a famous ancient statue of an athletic young man. It is the finest existing copy of the head of the original by Polyclitus, the fifth-century B.C. Greek sculptor who worked out a system of harmonious proportions of the human body. It is signed by a copyist named Apollonius of Athens, who lived in the first century B.C. In Roman times, fresh garlands of flowers may have hung on a hook in front of the bust, perhaps as a tribute to the athlete. The original statue was a full-length nude. Because of its balanced proportions, the original has become one of the most renowned sculptures of antiquity.

Elsewhere in the inner peristyle was found the head of an Amazon, a legendary woman warrior. Probably the oddest find was a portable bronze sundial fashioned in the shape of a ham.

The exit from the house outside to the grand courtyard (the main peristyle garden) led through a columned room. In this room, an archaic marble statue of the goddess Athena—a statue in the style of even earlier times—strikes a rather stiff and awkward pose. Bronze portrait busts were set in two rows. A portrait bust is a statue that shows the subject's head and shoulders. One of the busts is of a man with a shaved head. The

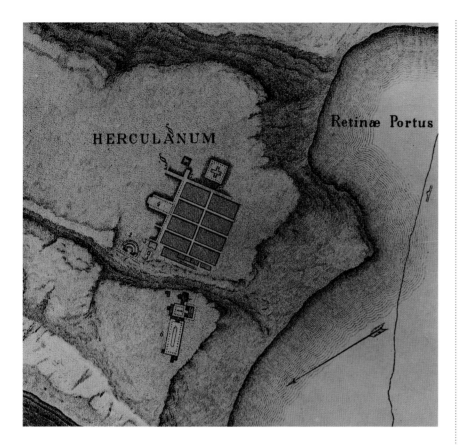

HERCULANUM

Retinæ Portus

An eighteenth-century map indicates the Villa of the Papyri's location: about 100 yards outside of the town walls of Herculaneum.

stubble of his hair appears as a kind of tattoo on the statue's skull. Scattered on the floor of this room were papyrus scrolls and wax tablets. Earth tremors may have dislodged them—or is it possible that they were dropped by an agitated Roman fleeing from Vesuvius with an armful of treasured books and documents?

Outside, the main peristyle garden overlooked the bay. In a rectangular arrangement some 330 feet long and 122 feet wide, sixty-five columns surrounded the courtyard. On one side, an enclosed, windowed walkway no doubt provided protection from the elements. In the center of the garden was a pond as large as the swimming pools in the Imperial Baths in Rome: 217 feet long and 23 feet wide. It may have been

Five bronze women, faithful copies of statues found in the Villa's main peristyle, surround the narrow pool of the museum's inner peristyle garden. These so-called *Dancing Maidens* are not really dancing, as was first thought. Some are performing the movements of drawing water and others may be dressing or undressing.

a fish pond or an ornamental pool that was sometimes used for swimming.

Enough sculptures were found here to supply a whole art gallery. It is believed that, concealed underground, an aqueduct and a complicated hydraulic system supplied the house, the ponds, and the fountains with water. At the end of a graveled pathway stood a small rotunda, a round garden house decorated with marble. It had a circular marble floor with triangular designs. The original floor is now on display in the Naples museum, for it was brought up piece by piece, and a copy of the floor can be seen at the Getty Museum.

The sculptures in the main peristyle garden are wonderfully executed and many have become famous. Some were original works of art; others were copies of masterpieces, created by copyists who were themselves masters.

In the garden, statues of two bronze deer, a jumping piglet, and various busts were displayed among flowers and shrubs. At a curve of the pool along one end, excavators found an extraordinary life-size bronze statue of a young naked faun (in myth a follower of the Roman wine-god Bacchus). The faun is shown dozing, with his right arm lazily thrown back over his head. Under thick, curly hair, short horns sprout from his forehead. From the sides of his cheeks dangle little goat wattles. The statue was probably placed so that its image would be reflected in the pool of water. It is considered one of the greatest sculptures of antiquity. But who was the sculptor? No one knows. There is no signature.

Under the columns were five life-size statues of young women. They each wear a simple Greek garment, the peplos, draped from their shoulders. The group is often called the *Dancing Maidens*, but actually the women are in positions for fetching water from a fountain-house. A fountain-house was a place to bathe, also, and some of the maidens appear to be dressing or undressing. Their eyes are made of white and colored glass paste. The edges of their bronze garments show traces of color. They are certainly more than 2,000 years old.

Still more sculptures adorned the garden. One marble is an earthy animal group, *Pan and a Goat*. It was intended to poke fun at the animal nature of man, although some people

A life-size bronze shows the Greek messenger-god Hermes (Romans called him Mercury) wearing the delicate winged sandals that enable him to fly. In the 1750s, tunnelers pulled the original *Hermes Resting* from the buried Villa. Today, this copy resides in a serene and elegant garden of the J. Paul Getty Museum that captures the feeling of an ancient Roman setting.

find it shocking because it depicts Pan (who is half-man and half-goat) mating with an animal. The most important sculptures in the garden were two boy runners or wrestlers, the *Drunken Faun,* and the world-famous *Hermes Resting.* All are of bronze, all life-size.

The runners or wrestlers are a pair of young naked boys about to begin the race or fight. For a look at them, turn to the photograph in Chapter 11 (page 124). Their eyes of glass paste seem real, and their lips show traces of red coloring. Their well-proportioned bodies are modeled with lifelike grace. The

Drunken Faun, however, portrays a once-athletic body in middle age. He lies drunk on an inflated wineskin. Raising himself on his left arm, he snaps the fingers of his right hand. He is laughing hilariously or singing, apparently letting everyone know that he is not old yet. Again, the sculptor is unknown.

An unquestioned masterpiece is the *Hermes Resting*, which has become familiar to many people thanks to reproductions displayed in Y.M.C.A.s, universities, and, of course, museums throughout the country. Young Hermes is shown naked except for winged sandals strapped to his ankles. Relaxed and graceful, he pauses for a moment on a rock before again taking flight as the messenger of the gods. (The Greeks knew him as Hermes; to the Romans, he was Mercury.) His lips, too, are touched with red.

From this one villa came about ninety pieces of sculpture, the largest collection of ancient bronze statuary ever found. When the Villa's statuary was brought above ground in the eighteenth century, superstitious peasants gathered around the tunnels' entrances. As the naked pagan "demons" appeared from the earth, the peasants crossed themselves in fear. No doubt, many more "demons" await. Copies of many Villa statues were made for display in Athens, home of great Greek sculpture. The originals were stolen by the German Nazis during World War ii, but have since been recovered.

As impressive as the Villa's statues are, they make up only part of this amazing story. Under Weber's direction, the eighteenth-century tunnelers toiled for more than two years before discovering what has become the Villa's most stunning contribution to the history of archaeology. In a small room, they found

The 2,000-year-old papyrus texts that give the Villa of the Papyri its name are now extremely fragile, as you can see from this charred fragment (right). About 1,800 books were found in the Villa's library, most of them written in Greek.

Roman books were written on papyrus scrolls like the one pictured in a wall painting from Herculaneum. Papyrus was a tough paperlike substance made from Egyptian reeds.

wooden shelves stacked with what appeared to be cylinder-shaped charcoal briquettes. At first, discoverers mistook the "briquettes" for pieces of wood or rolled-up fishing nets. But they turned out to be 1,787 badly scorched rolls of papyrus. This was the first ancient library ever discovered. Years later, the sands of Egypt and the Dead Sea caves would yield other ancient manuscripts, but in 1754, the Villa's collection of "books" was a first.

Despite the fact that the manuscripts seemed unreadable, the find excited the world. The problem was how to unroll the fragile scrolls and read them. In the eighteenth century, no methods existed for such a task. King Charles III called in a painter, whose efforts resulted in many scrolls being damaged and destroyed and only a few words made clear. The attempt was given up.

In 1753, a specialist in old manuscripts arrived from the Vatican in Rome. His name was Father Antonio Piaggio, and he set to work constructing a machine for unrolling the papyrus. It unwound a scroll at the rate of less than half an inch per hour. After four years of trial and error, the machine had unwound three scrolls. Scholars who had been waiting to examine the library's writings finally had something to read: part of the *Essay on Music* by a Greek philosopher named Philodemus.

Slowly, new scrolls were examined. So excited was the world that the king of England hired scholars to come to Italy and lend a hand. And such personages as Pope Pious IX and the czar of Russia visited Naples to see the books for themselves. Today, about 800 scrolls still remain unread.

In 1980, an international exhibition of the Villa's scrolls was held in Italy's great National Library, a former palace in Naples. Scholars and tourists came from all over the world to view them. The contents of some scrolls had been partially transcribed on copper plates to preserve them. Computer copies were made of others.

Almost ten years later, researchers using computer enhancement announced an important new discovery: a Greek translation of the story of Aeneas, the greatest work of the Latin poet Vergil. Until then, scholars had not known that Vergil had been translated into Greek.

Another new discovery was announced. Portions of *On the Nature of Things*, a famous work by the Roman poet and thinker Lucretius, had been found on two scrolls. Lucretius, who lived in the first century B.C. at about the same time as Julius Caesar, held some very advanced ideas for his time. For example, he believed that the gods did not exist. Most important was his theory that all matter was made up of atoms, and that atoms differed. He had many other ideas. He outlined the way mankind discovered the use of metals. He believed that humans had developed language because of their tongues—not, as others believed, tongues because of speech. The discovery of *On the Nature of Things* may help us learn even more about Lucretius and his teachings.

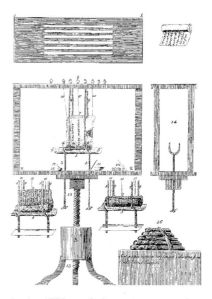

In the 1750s, an Italian priest created a special machine to unwind the brittle papyrus documents. It took four years to unroll just three books.

Most of the scrolls examined are the work of one man—the philosopher Philodemus. Most were in the Greek language; a few were in Latin. The hoped-for unknown writings of great classical masters were missing—a severe disappointment for everyone. How could the owner of so stupendous a villa have collected so narrow a library? It seemed likely that only the patron of a particular author would limit his entire library to the works of that single author.

This provides a clue about who may have owned the Villa. We know that a wealthy Roman named Lucius Calpurnius Piso was the patron and supporter of Philodemus. Piso's daughter, Calpurnia, was Julius Caesar's wife. So the Villa outside Herculaneum might have belonged to this Piso, or perhaps someone else in his family, and Julius Caesar may have visited there. These deductions are supported by one of Philodemus's poems, in which he calls himself Piso's "pet friend."

Much of the Villa is still untouched. Yet to be discovered are the living quarters and workrooms: the bedrooms, dining rooms, children's playrooms, kitchen, workshops, servants' quarters, garden sheds, boathouses. Try, if you can, to imagine what awaits us in those sealed rooms: the decorations, furniture, statuary, jewels, private articles, and all the gear necessary to the operation of a huge country estate.

Who could argue that amazing discoveries remain to be made in the Villa of the Papyri, now also called the Piso Villa by many people? Further excavations may prove the name.

Fortunately, the J. Paul Getty Museum now exists for everyone to see and enjoy. Businessman J. Paul Getty visited Herculaneum and became fascinated by the town. Because plans of the

Villa of the Papyri existed, Mr. Getty decided to use them as a basis for building a museum where he could exhibit his large collection of ancient Greek and Roman art. He brought in experts to accomplish the slow and difficult job. It took painstaking planning and two years of construction time. As a reward, visitors are as fascinated by the J. Paul Getty Museum as Mr. Getty was with the Villa at Herculaneum.

Success of the effort can be measured by the reaction of Giuseppe Maggi, Italian archaeologist. Dr. Maggi was formerly director of both the National Archaeological Museum in Naples and the excavations at Herculaneum. After his first visit he said, "I had, I confess, some suspicion that it would be a modern interpretation of the famous Villa of the Papyri, conforming only remotely to the ancient model. But . . . I felt an enormous emotion, not only from the perfect resemblance of the architecture, the lights and shadows of the peristyles, the original Villa's works of art, but also because one found the unique Villa of the Papyri, visible, alive with people, essentially the original."

Although the museum is not an exact replica of the Villa of the Papyri, most of the important known features of the ancient villa are re-created there. The museum has also drawn on the extensive remains of Herculaneum and Pompeii for many architectural details. When you arrive at the museum's main peristyle garden, you truly feel as if you are entering the Roman past. Like the original, the peristyle, a columned walkway, is well over 300 feet in length. You will see many of the same shrubs and flowers that Romans would have seen in a typical house or villa in Herculaneum. And you will see the same type of statuary and decorative objects, placed in the same type of setting.

Seen from above, a marble statue of Hercules holds a place of honor in the museum's Shrine of Hercules. The spectacular floor uses 4,000 pieces of antique marble to re-create the ancient floor of the Villa's rotunda. Although the floor is a replica of one from the Villa, the shrine itself is not. This room, based on an underground Roman tomb, was built by the museum to showcase Mr. Getty's favorite statue.

The main peristyle garden has the reflecting pool with the *Drunken Faun* at one end and the *Sleeping Faun* at the other. In between, you will find *Hermes Resting*, the bronze deer, and the boy runners or wrestlers. At the inner peristyle, the bronze maidens are placed around a narrow pool, where they appear to be busily drawing water.

Within, you can admire marbles of many colors brought from every corner of the old Roman world. Here, pieces of marble are set into the same intricate and beautiful patterns as they are in the original Villa and other Roman houses. Wall paintings from the houses of Herculaneum and Pompeii are reproduced here, and bronze ornaments and lamps are faithful castings of originals. When you enter the atrium, you will find it typical of a Roman house, with its rectangular opening in the ceiling and its pool below.

Of all the impressive settings in the museum, the domed Shrine of Hercules is the most spectacular. The floor is an exact reproduction of the original found in the rotunda of the Villa of the Papyri. It was taken up with great care and now can be walked on in the Naples Museum. It is set in twenty rings of ninety-six triangles of alternating color—a total of 4,000 individual pieces. One type of marble was brought from Turkey, another from Tunisia in North Africa.

The shrine was built to showcase a statue of Hercules depicting the hero-god with his characteristic club and lion skin. The Getty Museum's Hercules is distinguished by its dignity and nobility. It is said to have been found in the ruins of the Emperor Hadrian's "wonder-of-the-world" villa at Tivoli, outside of Rome. The statue passed into the hands of the English Lansdowne family in the eighteenth century, and then into the hands of Mr. Getty, and it was a favorite of his.

The J. Paul Getty Museum contributes a great deal to our understanding of Roman architecture and art. Such an understanding is important to us because so much of our civilization is based on classic, and especially Roman, foundations.

AFTERWORD

Across the gap of 2,000 years, the Town of Hercules offers us its precious gifts. But what does the future hold for them?

While wandering through the streets and buildings of Herculaneum, we have seen a treasure so great that it is hard to believe. Yet the most precious objects have not been left in the ancient town. They have been taken away from their original sites and placed under lock and key in museums.

One of these museums was in Herculaneum itself. It was an ordinary Herculaneum house called the Antiquarium. The big museum is in Naples and has been mentioned many times in this book. It is called the National Archaeological Museum. Built in 1586, it was originally a huge riding school for the aristocracy, and through the centuries has had different uses. Today it houses the world's most important collections from antiquity. These museums, plus the exhibitions at Pompeii, are true treasure troves.

Herculaneum's little museum held samples of some of the most valuable bronze and marble statuary, mosaics, and frescoes. But chiefly displayed were hundreds of small things.

The modern buildings of the town of Ercolano are sandwiched between the ancient homes of Herculaneum beneath them and the timeless profile of Vesuvius above them.

Here is a partial list: combs, mirrors, needles, earrings, beads of amber and glass, candelabra, oil lamps, a lantern of bronze and glass, double-pronged instruments for mending fishnets, wheat, beans, eggs, pistachio nuts, rope, baskets, part of a bed covering, fishnet, hinges, a bronze water valve, ink bottles, silver dishes, fishhooks, a carpenter's plane, a heap of nails, money, glass jars, seals, a surveyor's triangle, kitchen pots, wax tablets, amulets, flutes, brooches, rings of all sorts, perfume flasks, pins, a chariot wheel, spoons, weights, scales, medical instruments, and—of all things—a bowl of charred cookies baked with a flower pattern. A similar list of items in the Naples Museum would be almost endless.

Most of these objects were found during the period of helter-skelter tunneling that prevailed in the 1700s and 1800s, so in many cases a find's exact location is unknown. It is a pity not to know where a surveyor's triangle, medical instruments, or some of the exceptional jewelry were found. Imagine, as one example, a brooch so delicately carved that it compresses a whole Egyptian scene into a space smaller than a fingernail. Whose house did it come from? We simply don't know.

Small objects can be displayed well in museum cases, but furniture, frescoes, mosaics, and statuary are not shown to best advantage there. They were designed in relation to architecture—houses, temples, shops—not in the context of the blank rooms of a museum. Objects of art in a museum compete with one another in a way not intended by the artists. The cold light from fluorescent tubes in enormous dead-white chambers does a great disservice to a marble Apollo or Venus. It becomes harder to visualize the god or goddess in their original soft and glowing colors, set in a temple of brilliant reds, blues, and golds. What we see today is only a pale-gray likeness of the original.

Bronze statuary fares better, but without the original setting, much is lost.

As for the intricate mosaic floors that have been carried away and reset in museums, visitors walk over them with hardly a glance. The mosaicist's art is not fully appreciated. The same is true for wall paintings. They were created for individual rooms and were not meant to be lined up beside one another.

If the statuary, frescoes, mosaics, marble pavements, furniture, and personal objects must be taken from an ancient room to a modern museum, then why not move the room itself? Why not keep everything together as it was found? Why not preserve the whole house?

The better solution, of course, is the ideal goal of modern excavators: to leave every object, as far as possible, where it belongs. In this way, the excavation site itself becomes the museum—a living scene from a dead past. That past can then inform and enrich the present, and contribute to the education of people around the world.

In the 1990s, excavation at Herculaneum almost stopped. The Italian government no longer provided funds for regular exploration. Officials say that Italy has many archaeological sites—which it has—and to provide for them all is too costly. Funds are given for limited maintenance, such as repairs when roofs collapse. Clearly, houses as old as those in the Town of Hercules require more than normal attention.

Without funds, it has not been possible to train and keep a crew of skilled diggers. Instead, private excavating firms are called in for short-term jobs. Everyone admits that their methods and their workers are not well-suited to archaeology.

Another excavation force, a volunteer group, existed

for a while in the 1970s. Each summer, the "Herculaneum Academy" drew together archaeological students from many countries. They lived in a villa not far from the dig. They volunteered their services with pick and shovel and also sorted and classified potsherds. Students toiled steadily under the blistering sun, pitting their muscles against the damage done by Vesuvius. It was a cheering sight—young men and women taking seriously their responsibility to history. Unfortunately, this project was discontinued. Many people have expressed hope that it will resume.

Although excavation of Pompeii is nearly complete, digging continues on a large scale. Pompeii has become one of the major tourist attractions of Italy. It draws thousands of people every year. The excavation of Herculaneum, in contrast, has just begun.

Only four blocks of Herculaneum have been completely uncovered. How many more blocks exist? Of the important public buildings, only the Forum Baths are now entirely visible. Some rooms of the Suburban Baths are not yet cleared. Much of the Palaestra is hidden. The Basilica and the Theater are totally buried. The Villa of the Papyri remains underground, though its location once again is known. Other villas like it undoubtedly exist. We have only scratched the surface of Herculaneum thus far.

Archaeological digging today is much easier than in the past. Modern technology has added many impressive devices to the archaeologist's tool kit. For example, sonar—which helped re-locate the Villa of the Papyri—can help determine exactly where to dig. Computer enhancement of the text of some of the books found in the Villa's library, called "digital picture processing," is another high-tech tool. The necessity of using electronic warning devices to protect important frescoes is a sad commentary on human nature. Some people cannot resist the temptation to scribble their initials (like the Spanish tunnelers did in 1750) on any available surface. Now an outstretched arm with a pen can produce a shrill warning not to touch, and bring guards. At Pompeii, visitors use computers to ask the questions once asked of guards.

What will future excavations reveal? Will a small covered theater for poetry reading (like the Odeon in Pompeii) come to light? Did an amphitheater exist? What of a covered marketplace for selling fish and meat? Are the docks and piers still preserved under the pyroclastic flow? What of inns and taverns, town gates, the cemetery, and the temples, which surely must be impressive? Just imagine the paintings, statuary, tools, and household objects still locked in that Vesuvian stone. Do more libraries, in many ways the most precious finds of all, await us? How many more graffiti, those personal messages from the past, remain scribbled on walls? (Who can forget the schoolboy who painfully wrote out one of his daily lessons in its entirety? Or the girl who printed: "Hyacinthus was here. His Virginia salutes him.")

For the time being, the Italian government is spending its funds and energies on computerizing Pompeii. Herculaneum has been included, but to a lesser extent. In 1990, about $24 million was set aside for this project. Part of the project was to design a system for full exploration of the archaeological sites around Vesuvius. Another part was to set up virtual reality "walk-throughs" of important structures or streets. The first was a "visit" to the Stabian Baths at Pompeii. A "walk-through" of Herculaneum could be the next best thing to a visit there in person.

An Italian conservation organization has proposed that the area around Vesuvius be set aside as a national park, like the national parks in the United States. In this way, new construction at Ercolano would be limited or stopped, and archaeological sites protected. And in the future many lives might be saved when Vesuvius erupts again. Unfortunately, nothing has been done about the proposal.

Meanwhile, most of Herculaneum continues its 2,000-year-old sleep. Early in the twentieth century the English archaeologist Sir Charles Watson said: "Herculaneum is the one site above all others which ought to be excavated." And, more recently, the famed American archaeologist Dr. Frank E. Brown—then Director of the American Academy in Rome—added, "Herculaneum is probably archaeology's most flagrant unfinished business." Both were right. Nowhere else do we know of a time capsule quite like it waiting to be opened. If you found a buried treasure trove, wouldn't you want to dig up all of it?

GLOSSARY

A.D. *An abbreviation for the Latin words* Anno Domini, *which mean "in the year of the Lord." Used with dates to indicate a year after the beginning of the Christian era.*

adze *a cutting tool used for shaping wood.*

amphora *(plural: amphorae) A long, narrow* terra-cotta *jar with a pointed bottom and two small handles at the top. Used for storing or transporting liquids, such as wine, oil, or sauces. See also* dolium.

apse *A semicircular alcove, usually with a vaulted ceiling.*

aqueduct *A channel for transporting water to towns and cities, often over long distances. Sometimes arches were built to raise aqueducts above rivers or other obstacles.*

archaeology *The scientific study of ancient peoples—their artifacts and material remains.*

archaeological excavation *The process of digging up an ancient site.*

atrium *The main room or central hall of a Roman house.*

basilica *A public building for trying court cases and conducting business.*

B.C. *An abbreviation for the words "Before Christ." Used for dates before the beginning of the Christian era.*

caldarium *The hot room in Roman public baths.*

calends *In the Roman calendar, the first day of the month.*

centaur *A mythological creature that is half-man and half-horse.*

colonnade *A walkway or passage with rows of columns that support a roof. Often built around the perimeter of an outdoor courtyard. See also* peristyle, portico.

compluvium *A central opening in the roof of the* atrium *that lets light and rainwater enter. See also* impluvium.

cubiculum *(plural: cubicula) The bedroom of a Roman house.*

deify *To declare that someone or something has become a god or goddess. In Roman times, emperors and empresses were deified and worshiped.*

deity *A god or goddess.*

dig   An archaeological excavation.

dolium *(plural: dolia)   Large terra-cotta vessel or jug. Dolia filled with grain, nuts, and hot and cold foods were recessed in the countertops of Roman snack bars. See also* amphora.

fauces   *The narrow entrance or passage leading into a Roman* atrium *house. From the Latin word meaning "throat" or "jaws."*

faun   *In Roman mythology, a woodland creature usually shown as a man with one or more animal-like features, such as a small tail, small goat's horns, or wattles.*

Forum   *In Roman towns and cities, the civic center containing shops, public buildings, and temples.*

freedman/freedwoman   *A former slave who bought or was granted freedom.*

fresco *(plural: frescoes)   A wall painting created by applying colors or pigments to moist or dry plaster.*

frigidarium   *The cold room in Roman public baths.*

glowing avalanche   *A red-hot cloud of gases and volcanic ash created by an erupting volcano. Consists of a fast-moving, gaseous* surge *and a dense, ground-hugging* pyroclastic flow.

impluvium   *A rectangular pool in the* atrium *floor of a Roman house. Used to catch rainwater that entered through the* compluvium *located directly above it.*

insula *(plural: insulae)   An ancient city block made up of densely packed houses and shops.*

lararium   *A small shrine in a Roman house where the family worshiped the home's protecting spirits, the* lares *and* penates.

lares   *Roman household gods whose statues were placed in the home's shrine, or* lararium.

loggia   *A second-floor balcony or open room, usually overlooking a courtyard or the* atrium.

mosaic   *A picture made of many tiny pieces of colored stone or tile.*

Oscans   *First people known to live in the Bay of Naples region. In the 800s* B.C., *Oscans established a settlement on a site that later became Herculaneum.*

oscillum *(plural: oscilla)   A disc or mask hung between the columns in a* peristyle *garden, where it spun or oscillated in the breeze.*

palaestra   *A sports complex—gymnasium, playing field, swimming pool—where Romans exercised and competed in athletic events.*

papyrus   *A type of ancient "paper" made from Egyptian reeds. Usually rolled around a wooden spindle to form a scroll.*

patricians   *Upper-class Roman citizens.*

penates   *Roman household gods who looked after the family's well-being. They were worshiped in a small family shrine, the* lararium.

peristyle   *A garden courtyard surrounded by rows of columns. Typical of large, later-style Roman houses. See also* colonnade, portico.

plebeians   *Ordinary working-class people of Roman society.*

Plinian eruption   *A violent volcanic event that throws hot gas, ash, pumice, and rock fragments many miles into the air in the form of a huge, mushroom-shaped cloud. Named for Pliny the Younger, an eyewitness who graphically described Mount Vesuvius's* A.D. *79 eruption.*

portico   *A porch with a roof supported by columns. See also* colonnade, peristyle.

potsherds   *Bits of broken pottery found during* archaeological excavations.

proconsul   *The title of an important government official or military commander of a Roman province.*

pyroclastic flow   *In a volcanic eruption, the dense, ash-laden portion of a glowing avalanche. Pyroclastic flow deposits over whelmed and buried the Town of Hercules to a depth of up to 65 feet.*

relief   *Three-dimensional scenes and figures carved into the flat surface of a stone.*

Samnites   *A tribe of Italic people who invaded the Bay of Naples region in the 400s B.C. They were the dominant power until their defeat by Rome in the first century B.C.*

satyr   *In Greek and Roman myths and plays, a woodland creature depicted as a human being with some goatlike features, such as hooves or shaggy hair.*

sesterce   *An ancient Roman silver coin.*

solarium *(plural: solaria)   A sun room or uncovered terrace at the side or rear of a Roman house.*

strigil   *A curved metal or bone scraper for removing oil and grime from a person's skin. Used by Romans to clean themselves at the public baths.*

stucco   *A hard, slow-setting plaster, often used in Roman buildings to create decorative details.*

stylus   *A long, sharp tool used for writing on* wax tablets.

surge   *In a volcanic eruption, the hot, fast-moving phase of a glow-ing avalanche. Scientists believe that surges are what killed most victims of the A.D. 79 eruption of Mount Vesuvius.*

tablinum   *A room in a Roman home located behind the* atrium. *In older houses, it was the bed-room of the owner of the house; by A.D. 79, it was generally used as a reception room for meeting clients and guests.*

tepidarium   *The warm room in Roman public baths.*

terra-cotta   *A reddish-brown clay used for pottery vases, jugs, statuettes, and other objects.*

thermae   *The Latin word for the public baths.*

thermopolium *(plural: thermopo-lia)   A Roman snack bar or tav-ern serving hot and cold food and wine.*

triclinium   *The dining room of a Roman house.*

tufa   *A type of volcanic rock commonly found in the Vesuvius area.*

villa   *A large country house with beautiful gardens, or a wealthy family's farming estate.*

volcanologist   *A scientist who specializes in the study of volca-noes.*

wax tablets   *Wax-covered wooden boards. In ancient times, people wrote on them by scratch-ing the wax with a* stylus.

INDEX

PHOTOGRAPH CREDITS

frontis: Soprintendenza Archeologica delle Province di Napoli e Caserta; *viii:* Jonathan Blair; *4:* Scala/Art Resource, NY; *5 left:* Lorenzo Loli, Infant Hercules with Snakes, Graphische Sammlung Albertina; *5 center:* The J. Paul Getty Museum; *5 right:* DAI; *8:* Erich Lessing/Art Resource, NY; *10:* The American Numismatic Society; *11 top:* L. Pedicini, Naples; *12 right:* DAI; *13:* Soprintendenza Archeologica delle Province di Napoli e Caserta; *14 bottom:* Michael Grant, Cities of Vesuvius: Pompeii & Herculaneum; *16:* Pierre-Henri, Valenciennes La Mort du Plin, Musée des Augustins, Toulouse; *18 top:* Roger Viollet; *18 bottom:* Ron and Nancy Goor, Pompeii: Exploring a Roman Ghost Town; *21:* Stock Montage; *28:* American Numismatic Society; *35:* United States Department of the Interior, US Geological Survey, David A. Johnston, Cascades Volcano Observatory, Vancouver, WA; *37:* Amedeo Maiuri, Herculaneum; *40:* Museo del Prado; *41 right:* Trustees of the Wedgwood Museum, Barlaston, Staffordshire, England; *42:* Leonard von Matt; *45 left:* Museo Nazionale, Napoli, Soprintendenza Archeologica delle Province di Napoli e Caserta; *45 right:* DAI; *48:* Kurt Hauser; *50:* Kurt Hauser; *52:* Soprintendenza Archeologica di Pompeii; *53:* Soprintendenza Archeologica di Pompeii; *54:* J.B. Ward-Perkins, Pompeii A.D. 79: Treasures from the National Archaeological Museum, Naples, and the Pompeii Antiquarium; *55 top:* J.B. Ward-Perkins, Pompeii A.D. 79: Treasures from the National Archaeological Museum, Naples, and the Pompeii Antiquarium; *55 bottom:* Theodor Kraus (*text*) and Leonard von Matt (*photography*), Lebendiges Pompeii und Herculaneum, DuMont Buchverlag, Köln 1973; *56 left top:* Museo Nazionale Romano, photo: A. De Luca, Rome; *56: left bottom:* L. Pedicini, Naples; *56 right center:* Museo Nazionale, Napoli, Soprintendenza Archeologica delle Province di Napoli e Caserta; *58:* Museo Nazionale; *59:* Soprintendenza Archeologica di Pompeii; *60:* Marcel Brion, Pompeii & Herculaneum: The Glory and the Grief; *62:* Jonathan Blair; *64:* O. Louis Mazzatenta, @ National Geographic Society; *67 top:* Foglia, Naples; *67 center:* Cheryl Nuss, @ National Geographic Society; *67 right:* Museo Nazionale, Naples, photo: Foglia, Naples; *70:* Jonathan Blair; *71:* Jonathan Blair; *72:* Jonathan Blair; *73:* C.M. Dixon; *74:* Eugen Kusch Herculaneum, Verlag Hans Carl, Nürnberg; *75:* J.B. Ward-Perkins, Roman Architecture, Electa, Milano; *77:* Amedeo Maiuri, Ercolano: I Nuovi Scavi (1927–1958); *78:* Soprintendenza Archeologica delle Province di Napoli e Caserta; *79:* photo: L. Pedicini, Naples; *80 top:* Museo Nazionale, Naples, photo: L. Pedicini, Naples; *80 bottom:* Soprintendenza Archeologica delle Province di Napoli e Caserta; *81 top:* Museo Nazionale, Naples, Soprintendenza Archeologica delle Province di Napoli e Caserta; *81 center:* Museo Nazionale, Naples, Soprintendenza Archeologica delle Province di Napoli e Caserta; *83:* Soprintendenza Archeologica delle Province di Napoli e Caserta; *87 top:* Museo Nazionale, Naples, Soprintendenza Archeologica delle Province di Napoli e Caserta; *88:* Soprintendenza Archeologica delle Province di Napoli e Caserta; *89:* Alinari/Art Resource, NY; *90:* SEF/Art Resource, NY; *92:* Museo Archeologico Nazionale, photo: L. Pedicini, Naples; *96:* Soprintendenza Archeologica delle Province di Napoli e Caserta; *97:* Amedeo Maiuri, Ercolano: I Nuovi Scavi (1927–1958); *99 bottom:* Museo Nazionale, Naples, Soprintendenza Archeologica delle Province di Napoli e Caserta; *100:* Soprintendenza Archeologica delle Province di Napoli e Caserta; *101 left:* Soprintendenza Archeologica di Pompeii; *101 center top:* DAI; *101 center bottom:* Soprintendenza Archeologica delle Province di Napoli e Caserta; *103:* Soprintendenza Archeologica delle Province di Napoli e Caserta; *104:* Fototeca Unione; *106:* Museo Archeologico Nazionale, Naples, photo: L. Pedicini, Naples; *112:* Museo Nazionale, photo: L. Pedicini, Naples; *114:* Amedeo Maiuri, Ercolano: I Nuovi Scavi (1927–1958); *117:* Soprintendenza Archeologica delle Province di Napoli e Caserta; *118:* Soprintendenza Archeologica delle Province di Napoli e Caserta; *120:* Marcel Brion, Pompeii and Herculaneum: The Glory and the Grief; *123:* Soprintendenza Archeologica di Napoli e Caserta; *126:* Amedeo Maiuri, Ercolano: I Nuovi Scavi (1927–1958); *128:* Marcel Brion, Pompeii and Herculaneum: The Glory and the Grief; *131:* Soprintendenza Archeologica di Napoli; *132:* Amedeo Maiuri, Ercolano: I Nuovi Scavi (1927–1958); *134 right:* Scala/Art Resource, NY; *135:* Michael Grant, Cities of Vesuvius: Pompeii & Herculaneum; *137:* DAI; *138:* Amedeo Maiuri, Ercolano: I Nuovi Scavi (1927–1958); *140:* Scala/Art Resource, NY; *142:* Scala/Art Resource, NY; *143:* Alinari/Art Resource, NY; *144:* Soprintendenza Archeologica delle Province di Napoli e Caserta; *148:* Foglia, Naples; *150:* Alinari/Art Resource, NY; *151:* Amedeo Maiuri, Ercolano: I Nuovi Scavi (1927–1958); *152:* Aliniari, Firenze; *153 top:* Robert Harding Picture Library; *153 center:* DAI; *156:* The J. Paul Getty Museum; *158 top:* O. Louis Mazzatenta, @ National Geographic Society; *158 bottom:* DAI; *159:* The J. Paul Getty Museum; *160:* Museo Archeologico Nazionale, Naples, photo: L. Pedicini, Naples; *162:* The J. Paul Getty Museum; *164:* The J. Paul Getty Museum; *166 top:* O. Louis Mazzatenta, @ National Geographic Society; *166 bottom:* Museo Archeologico Nazionale, photo: L. Pedicini, Naples; *170:* The J. Paul Getty Museum; *172:* Kurt Hauser

DATE DUE